Eileen Ford's Book of Model Beauty
Secrets of the Model's World

Eileen Ford's

A

More Beautiful You in 21 Days

Illustrations by Richard Giglio

SIMON AND SCHUSTER · NEW YORK

Published by Simon and Schuster
Rockefeller Center, 630 Fifth Avenue
New York, New York 10020

SECOND   PRINTING

SBN 671-21191-9
Library of Congress Catalog Card Number: 72-80689
Designed by Edith Fowler
Manufactured in the United States of America

I wish to thank Joanne Dabney, my helper in the kitchen. She and I have worked together on these recipes for a long time. We worked them out together, eliminating the bad and reveling in the good.

Further thanks are due to Isabel Howard, mother of our model Angela Howard. She carefully counted calories and carbohydrates, divided and multiplied so that I could be sure of every word I have said.

Thanks to Lacey Ford, Jamie Ford, Katie Ford, Cathy Barber and Carolyn Beck, who helped me test the exercises and makeup tricks.

This book would not exist without my children's and friends' assistance. I hope they will always know how grateful I am.

Finally, a very special thank-you to Jack David, who has served the recipes to us and our guests with such a warm smile and such great good humor that even if I had made a mistake, the food would have tasted good anyhow.

This book is dedicated to all the women in the world who find themselves at their wits' end trying to cope with approaching, or already arrived, middle age. Extra fat, extra flab and somehow drab—living in a world of young people. "Apprehensive" and "anxious" are words that describe you now. I know: I was one of you.

But with this book in hand you can forget your fears. This book can and will remake you in three short weeks. A new face and figure are here for you. It's remarkably easy—you'll enjoy every minute of care you give yourself and every mouthful you eat.

This book is dedicated to the making of a confident, self-assured you. A new life is yours, starting today!

Contents

CONTENTS

Foreword

Imagine being the head of the world's most famous model agency and waking up to find yourself over forty and overweight! Not only overweight but, to tell the absolute truth about myself, I was in miserable shape. I don't mean to say that I was fat, but I wasn't thin —I wasn't even slender!

To be constantly surrounded by the most beautiful young girls in the world, to have a devastatingly good-looking husband and to find myself beginning to look the way I have always criticized women my age for looking . . . how had it happened? How could I have allowed myself to fall into the trap that I have known about, written about and spoken about for years? I honestly can't give you a good reason. We travel a lot, entertain a great deal at home and out—but more than that, I love to eat.

Out of shape is insidious. I had allowed myself to creep from a size 8 to size 10, and when pants really became an important fashion point I found that size-12 pants were becoming too snug to wear. To make matters worse, my husband had gone on a diet while I was away on a two-week business trip. He had lost about twenty pounds, had let his hair grow longer, had ordered new clothes and looked better than he had looked when we got married twenty-five years ago! All the models were talking about it!

Becoming overweight doesn't just happen overnight. It's something you allow to happen slowly, innocently . . . and all at once there you are, bulgy and old—old before your time; and I, Eileen Ford, had fallen into the comfortable trap.

When it came to me that awful, awful day of reckoning, I faced a lot of truths. In spite of talking to anyone who would listen about exercise, I myself had ceased to exercise more than a year before, giving myself the usual excuse about being too busy. I was a mass of flab; starting at the top and all the way to the bottom, I was like jelly. The difficulty of obtaining a cook had forced me to spend a great deal of time in the kitchen. Being an Aries, I am impelled to do everything I do better than anyone else, so I took up cooking with a passion. It may sound brazen, but I really became as good a cook as most chefs in New York's best restaurants. As we travel a great deal, I learned the best dishes of all the countries we know and love. Unfortunately, *I* was my biggest cooking fan. I ate everything I cooked, and lots of it! Foolish Eileen Ford!

The combination of good food in unrestricted content and amount and no exercise did exactly what you might expect it would do!

Then one day, one awful day, the voice of the seamstress at the couturier from whom I order my clothes saying, "Hips, thirty-eight inches" sounded like the death knell. That was the moment that changed my life—and I hope that it will become the moment that will change yours.

I am going to tell you the simple way in which I lost sixteen pounds in three weeks plus two inches from my waist and three from my hips. Now I've got firm thighs, a bikini-shaped tummy and a new lease on life. I'm no older-looking than my husband (who exercises religiously). I wear size-8 slacks and love it! So can you. You've got to care. Every woman has to care, deep down inside—but is afraid to try for fear her trying won't work. Diet and exercise can and will work. They did for me, and they will for you.

I also embarked on a crash beauty program. That is to say, I put into action a program that made me utilize all the knowledge I had and wasn't using. I practiced putting on my false eyelashes, how to use my hairpieces, applying false nails where needed. In other words, I pulled myself back together.

Maybe you have never set yourself a beauty goal; maybe you have and failed. Or worse, you could be like me and have allowed marriage and/or career to trap you into ignoring the basic facts of life. Every woman owes it to herself and everyone around her either to look better than she does or, if all is perfection, to maintain the status quo.

If you are in good shape and satisfied that you do not need any changes, then you do not need this book (unless you want some great recipes). However, if you need help—here it is! A new face, a new figure are yours for the reading and the doing. Three weeks—twenty-one days—changed my life as they will change yours.

In evolving my plan for diet and exercise, I had to face two facts: one, I hate to exercise; two, I love to eat. To cater to both sloth and gourmandise was difficult, but I did it! If you will follow my exercises, which seldom make you get off your back, and my diet, which offers recipes that will keep you and your husband and friends not just happy—ecstatic!—you will bless me the rest of your life.

P.S.: Although this book is dedicated to you, it will work for your husband or daughters, too! If they need it, you owe it to them to make sure they read it and follow this beauty plan.

Preface

Of all life's pleasures, nothing to me is more soothing, more sensuous, more satisfying than eating. I can eat anything at any time and be happy. Food is solace; food is the fuel that runs the engine that is our body, and good food, really good food, goes beyond the mere fact of eating. Good food is one of the sources of a happy life!

I often think with pity of the people who spend their lives eating the same old pieces of fried meat, overcooked vegetables and soggy salads. Life surely has to be more than that. It also has to be more than the good, nutritious food I was served as a child. Until my marriage to a food-loving New Orleanian, I never knew that there was more to eating than broiled steak, chops, chicken or roast meats flavored only with salt and accompanied only by plain vegetables. In my home, cake, cookies and hot breads dripping with butter were also present, as were homemade lollipops, fudge, chocolates and ice cream. We ate exceedingly well, but it was, number one, boring, and number two, fattening.

I lost my taste for sweets in the dentist's chair. At one point in my life, I went to the dentist once a week from April until November. From that time on, I have viewed sweets as a major

17

threat rather than a delight. My entire family had teeth riddled with cavities, and we all learned better the hard way. Therefore, sweets have not been a fattening factor in my life for many years.

I gained my real passion for eating when I first tasted Chinese food. It was the only thing I had ever eaten that varied from my normal diet. It was also the beginning of my tasting all the good foods of the world.

When finally model-agency business took Jerry and me to France, Italy, Germany, Sweden, Finland, Denmark, Spain and Australia, it was a revelation. The food was fantastic! The many mouth-watering ways in which food was prepared staggered my taste buds and left me permanently hungry. I could never wait to get back to each place where we had been to taste again the food we had enjoyed there. I loved the fresh breads, such as hot brioches with farm-fresh butter in Paris and Finn crisp with cheese in Helsinki; these are but two ways to start the day in Europe. Fettuccini dripping with cream and cheese in Rome, tiny new potatoes with dill and butter in Stockholm, pork stuffed with apples and prunes in Copenhagen and fresh foie gras in flaky pastry in Paris are all among the great dishes of their countries. There are myriad others equally good—equally fattening. I ate them all with enthusiasm. These delicacies, coupled with the fact that as a businesswoman I must lunch with clients almost daily, slowly and insidiously took their toll. A few ounces here, a pound there all added up to one fact: overweight.

When I finally could no longer close my eyes to the fact that I was overweight, I searched desperately for ways to circumvent the realities of the situation. I had to diet. But how could I diet and yet eat the way I loved to? Diet is a pain. Food is great. These facts had to be resolved from my own point of view. More than that, I know a great deal about nutrition and have always believed in the perfect balanced diet. When I approached forty, none of my perfect formulas for losing weight worked. Drastic measures were needed. I did not ask my doctor. She might have said, "Poppycock!" But if you do what I did, you should consult your doctor first. I did it without my doctor because I had to, and it worked. But everyone is different, and you should have a go-ahead from your physician.

As a lecturer on diet I know many kinds of diet and a great deal about calories and carbohydrates, and I decided to formulate a diet for myself that would seldom exceed the 50 or 60 grams of carbohydrate allowed daily on a low-carbohydrate diet. I further decided that calories do indeed count and made this fact very much a part of my thinking. Then I began to search through my notes on foods I had eaten all over the world and looked feverishly for recipes that not only tasted good but fulfilled all of my requirements. Gradually it became clear to me that the perfect foods to satisfy all these requirements were fish and shellfish. So I made myself a diet that included only that. However, I cooked my fish and shellfish in an astonishing number of delicious ways—so many that I never really knew I was on a diet.

I emphatically would not recommend staying on this diet for longer than three weeks. The body needs the minerals and vitamins found in fresh fruit and vegetables. However, I have lost a lot of my taste for most meats. Fish is infinitely more delicate, and there are so many good ways to prepare it. When I do eat meat, it is very lean.

Knowing that I would miss Vitamin C by eliminating my daily grapefruit, I developed the habit of taking 1,000 units of Vitamin C and one therapeutic multiple-vitamin capsule with minerals daily. I also drank eight glasses of water or iced tea with lemon daily. There are many diets that say you can drink low-calorie sodas. I believe that you should not, as carbonated drinks puff you up and are not necessary at all. The liquid is an essential part of my diet—you must not ignore one single glass of liquid.

I included the liquid in my diet by having two glasses of iced tea with lemon at nine-thirty and eleven-thirty in the morning. I had two more glasses at four in the afternoon. I do not think anyone needs a cocktail at lunch. It blurs the mind and is very fattening.

If I found myself hungry between meals, I ate one of those shrimp cocktails that you can buy in any delicatessen. There are times, I confess, when I felt I might float away; but I didn't, and my insides functioned. My skin was clear, and the enormous amounts of protein that I consumed gave me fast energy.

Jerry Ford and I have never eaten better than we did on this diet. In fact, Jerry didn't know that we were on one (not that he needed it, having already lost his excess weight). He did and does love the food I serve, and the recipes you will see on the following pages still form a major portion of our diet. This is through choice as well as the desire to maintain our contours and newfound zest for living.

You will see that all recipes are in quantities for *one* person. It is very easy to multiply if you wish to cook for more people. On the other hand, I've always found division difficult; that's why I made the recipes for a single serving. I must confess that preparing bouillabaisse for one is stretching it a bit; the more the merrier when you eat that glorious dish.

The day you start on this diet combined with the exercises and beauty plan is the day you open the door to a new life. If it worked for one overworked, middle-aged mother of four, believe me, it *can* work for you!

20

First Week

. . . The Awful Truth

Fill this in and read on!

WEIGHT	BUST	WAIST	HIPS	THIGHS
	37	29	39	22½

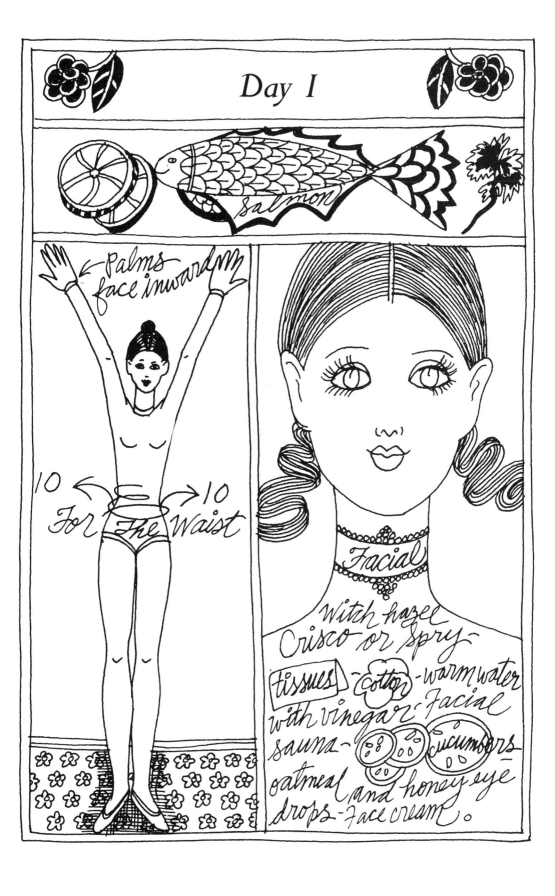

Day I

salmon

Palms face inward

10 ← → 10
For The Waist

Facial

Witch hazel — Crisco or Spry — tissues — cotton — warm water with vinegar — Facial sauna — cucumbers — oatmeal and honey — eye drops — face cream.

Menu

Breakfast

    1,000 units of Vitamin C and 1 therapeutic multiple-vitamin capsule with minerals

    8 cold boiled shrimp—large size most filling

    Tea or coffee without cream, milk or sugar

Lunch

    Jellied consommé with freshly ground pepper and a few drops of lemon juice

    1 or 2 pieces broiled flounder

    Tea or coffee without cream, milk or sugar

Dinner

    Shrimp cocktail (6 large size with bottled cocktail sauce)

    Broiled 4-oz. salmon steak with parsleyed margarine

    1 or 2 glasses dry white wine if desired

    Tea or coffee without cream, milk or sugar

Reminder: This diet must include eight glasses of liquid per day. This can include hot tea and coffee or iced tea and coffee or plain water and can be drunk with meals and at 9:30 A.M., 11:30 A.M. and 4:00 P.M.

Broiled Fillet of Flounder

2 slices flounder fillet
4 tbs. margarine
4 tbs. white wine
salt, pepper

Preheat oven to 350° for 20 minutes. Cream together margarine and wine. Wash fish and gently pat dry; sprinkle with salt and freshly ground pepper to taste. Brush a small amount of margarine mixture on one side of flounder and place fish on the broiling pan with this side three or four inches from the flame. Broil for about 20 minutes, basting with the margarine mixture. Fish will be done when it flakes easily with a fork. If you wish, you may add an extra teaspoon of margarine mixture when the fish is done.

Broiled Salmon Steak with Parsleyed Margarine

1 salmon steak 1 ½ inches thick
2 tbs. margarine
1 tbs. chopped parsley
salt

Preheat oven to 350° for 20 minutes. Cream together margarine and parsley. Wash fish and gently pat dry; sprinkle with salt and freshly ground pepper to taste. Brush a small amount of margarine mixture on top side of salmon steak and place the fish on the broiling pan three or four inches from the flame. Broil for about 20 minutes, basting with the margarine mixture. Fish will be done when it flakes easily with a fork. If you wish, you may add an extra teaspoon of margarine mixture when the fish is done.

Today is the best day you've had in a long time! Why? Because today you're going to start on my exercise program, and in three weeks there's going to be a brand-new you! If only I could tell you how I felt and how I feel, show you how I looked and how I look, you too would be as excited as I am for you. I know what a difference there's going to be mentally, physically —every which way.

For years I exercised—first this, then that group of exercises. Some worked, some didn't; some hurt, some didn't; they were all difficult. However, they all had one thing in common: after a week or two they became very boring. It's miserable to do the same thing day after day, week after week. Eventually, you're just bound to give up. Finally, when I decided to really put myself back in shape, I analyzed my feelings about exercise. I realized that tedium combined with sore muscles and lack of results was what stopped me each time. So I put together groups of exercises that gradually, painlessly (and now effortlessly) began to reshape me. More than that, I changed the exercises, even if just slightly, daily. I never had to do the exact same thing every day; therefore, I was not only not bored: I worked up a curiosity for what I would do each day and looked forward to the next group of exercises.

For additional benefit, I concentrated on breathing deeply as I was doing the exercises. My speech coach, Betty Cashman, had shown me some deep-breathing tricks that had reduced my waistline magically. Practitioners of yoga have known for years that deep breathing speeds the rate of oxidation (and therefore the metabolic rate), thus burning calories at a greater rate than occurs during ordinary breathing. I know two photographers, Dennis Reichle and Jean Pierre Zacharaison, who practice deep breathing when exercising. Both of them have very lean, hard bodies.

So, with this in mind, I incorporated deep breathing into all my exercises.

Starting on an exercise program is akin to giving up smoking: it takes self-determination. But if you have decided that you really want to look great, it's well worth the effort—and finally you'll find it's fun watching your body change. It's a challenge that you and you alone can meet!

I've heard it said that you must exercise at the same time every day. I'm not sure that it's true for you. It is for me because I can find the time only by getting up a half hour earlier every day. At the beginning, desperation was the catalyst. Today, pride keeps me going. I love to hear my friends say, "I can't get over how great you look." At any age a compliment never hurts and I get lots of them.

Furthermore, I feel wonderful, full of energy—so full that it's hard to describe how almost buoyant I feel. I had a physical check-up after my 21-day beauty regime and my doctor was really astonished to find that I was in such good condition. That's rewarding too.

I have to add a word of caution about my exercises. Take it

easy! Some of them are hard; if you can't really do them well, don't fret. Your body is a machine that has to be tuned like a motor. Take a half hour or an hour, according to your capacity. Every three weeks repeat the cycle. Eventually, you'll find that exercises you could not do at all have become simple. That's a promise. I still haven't really mastered every one, but that's a challenge. It's the fun. It'll keep you going for years to come. It will keep firming and toning your body the rest of your days.

Now is the time for you to start! Open the book flat on the floor beside you. Begin! Once you do, you're on your way to a great new you!

Exercise One / To Limber Up

Lie on stomach, hands at sides, chin on floor. Inhale. Slowly and smoothly lift your head and shoulders and turn your head to the right. Try to see your left foot, but do not strain your neck. Return slowly to original position, exhaling as you do. Repeat, and this time turn your head to the left, trying to see right foot. Repeat on each side 10 times.

Exercise Two / For the Waist

Standing erect, raise arms straight over head, palms facing inward. Inhale and bend slowly to the right, as far as is comfortable. Exhale as you bend. Be sure to keep arms parallel as you do this exercise. Return to upright position, inhaling as you do. Now bend to left repeating this same movement. Repeat 10 times on each side. You will find gradually that you can bend almost completely sideways from the waist.

Exercise Three | For Abdomen and Thighs

Lie on back on floor. Bend knees and raise legs with soles of feet parallel to floor. Clasp hands around legs. Inhale deeply and slowly as you contract abdomen and pull knees as close as possible to chest. Hold for a count of 3. Relax and exhale. Repeat 10 times, working up to 20.

Exercise Four | For Back

Lie on back on floor, feet on floor about thirty-six inches apart, toes pointing out, knees bent. Raise your arms over your head, elbows bent, and place your hands beside your head, palms down, fingers pointing toward your toes. Keeping shoulders and head on floor, inhale, press down on your feet and raise your buttocks from floor, exhaling as you do. Hold for a count of 3. Slowly inhale as you sink back into original position. Repeat 10 times and work up to 20.

Exercise Five | To Stretch

Stand up straight. Inhale as you rise up on the ball of your right foot and reach for heaven with your left arm. Exhale as you return. Now inhale as you rise up on the ball of your left foot and reach for the sky with your right arm. Repeat the two movements 10 times.

Exercise Six / For Circulation

Trot slowly in place, bouncing on balls of feet. Breathe quickly in and out 20 times.

I've got to assume that you really care as much as I did about remaking yourself; therefore, I have just said today is *the* most important day that's come along in a long time. You've started on a tremendous program of diet and exercise. Diet doesn't take any time; exercise takes between twenty and thirty minutes of your life today and every day of your life forever. But what about the rest of you—your face, your hands, your hair? What about them?

A few years ago, I wrote *Eileen Ford's Book of Model Beauty*. It's a good book which contains a wealth of general knowledge. If you are a complete novice in the world of beauty you should read it, for all the basics are there. Today, I'm going to start you on a postgraduate course in beauty. I'm going to answer the questions most frequently asked of me by women who really care.

If I ask you, "Do you *really* care?" the answer is going to come back "Yes." But do you really care enough to take the time to perfect yourself? You are the only person who can do it for you. I can tell you "how," but you've got to do it yourself—and why not try?

We live in a selfish world. People will take from you what they can get. The most precious thing (beyond the deep spiritual things) that any of us has is time. Everyone is willing to accept whatever time you can or will give to whatever thing it is that that person wants of you. You can cook—that takes time; make beds; go to the butcher, baker and bank. Nobody will thank you because all it took was time—your time. Your whole life is time. Seconds, minutes, hours, days are your life, and if you don't use them wisely you've wasted *your* life. Don't do it! Take the time it takes to take care of yourself. People really will appreciate you more. I'm not saying to forget your obligations —not at all. I am saying that you must save a little of your precious possession for yourself.

Be appreciated! Be admired! Be completely feminine and alluring. Don't let all the roving eyes go to someone else. Concentrate on yourself a little bit every day. The dividends are vast. Self-esteem is what you've lost. Self-esteem is what I'm hoping to make you regain. You—yes, you—can develop into the woman you never were, once were or always wanted to be by making yourself think like a WOMAN and by knowing the tricks that the beautiful women of the world know.

Just remember, it takes concentration—concentration on you! Then, and only then, will you be the woman you've yearned to be.

When you read these tricks, you'll see what I mean. The trick to being a real woman is to *know* the tricks and put them into practice. The key is concentration—concentration on the whole of you. Body, face, hair, hands, eyes—the whole of you needs concentration.

I have told you that the next three weeks will change your life, and they will: you're going to wake up and live! Live your life to its fullest.

A lithe, sinuous body; a glowing face; sexy eyes, hands, even feet; and hair that moves are yours starting now. This is *your* moment; seize it while you may. Believe in me and yourself. Together we're going a long, long way!

Beauty Tip

The Feminine Face

Every day one reads something about the beautiful people, and as their work is my world, I always give it close attention. And there is always one thing that strikes me: beautiful women, the world over, give time to every part of their bodies. Why not you? No reason. You've embarked on this program and you're going to start with your face.

What have you done for your face lately? Is it clean? Of course it is. Do you slap some moisture on it daily? Naturally. But what else?

When men look at women admiringly, do you for one minute think that all they see is a nice, clean face? If you do, you're really wrong. When a man looks at a woman's face, he's looking at her skin for one thing, and unless he sees skin that is glowing and that looks firm to the touch, he's likely to look at other skin.

I'm going to assume that you cleanse your face thoroughly and moisturize daily, and now will tell you what you can do once a week to give that nice, clean face of yours something special. Youthfully glowing, soft to the touch—that's what your face will become starting now.

In order to achieve your goal of lovelier skin, you must give yourself a weekly facial. Not a facial full of wildly expensive creams. What you need is a facial that will cleanse and refine your pores, tighten the muscles and stimulate circulation—and it can be quite inexpensive.

You will need:

1. A can of Spry or Crisco
2. Facial tissues
3. A bowl of warm water with one tsp. of vinegar
4. A facial sauna
5. A paste made of oatmeal and honey
6. Cotton pads
7. Witch hazel
8. 4 slices of cucumber
9. Eye drops
10. Face moisture

Start by cleansing your skin with Spry or Crisco. You read it correctly. Spry or Crisco is wonderful for cleansing the skin. Apply once and tissue off. Apply a second time and allow it to remain a few minutes. During this time try to touch your tongue to the tip of your nose twenty times. You won't succeed, but you will tighten the muscles under your chin. (You can do this daily with incredible results.) Now tissue off the second application of cleanser. Use cotton pads saturated in warm water mixed with a teaspoonful of vinegar to remove the rest of the cleanser. If your skin is very sensitive, use warm water alone. Your face is clean. So what? Read on and you'll see.

The next step is to use a facial sauna. It is not very expensive to purchase, and it is essential to my skin plan. Use it exactly according to the directions, and when your skin is very hot, take a tissue and gently press on any clogged pores to remove the dirt and oils that have accumulated. Then, with cupped hands, rinse thirty times with cool water.

Following the steaming your face will need a mask to close the pores and tighten the skin. There are many masks on the market. I make my own because it's lots cheaper and a great deal more interesting. Sometimes I combine oatmeal and honey into a paste and spread it on my face; other times I just beat up one egg and let it set for fifteen minutes on my face. You can feel the skin tighten. Then I rinse the whole thing off with luke-warm followed by cool water.

While you've got the mask on your face, put cotton pads soaked in witch hazel and then wrung out on your eyelids.

The final step is to go over your entire face with a few slices of cucumber. It's a fresh, new, lively feeling. Apply moisture cream, then a few eye drops, and the deed is done!

Look in the mirror. There's a difference. The skin that you want is starting to show through. But you won't achieve a miracle the first day. You've got to keep up these facials once a week forever.

If other women are doing it, why not you? The feminine face starts here—and if you want to know what to do with it, read on.

Day II

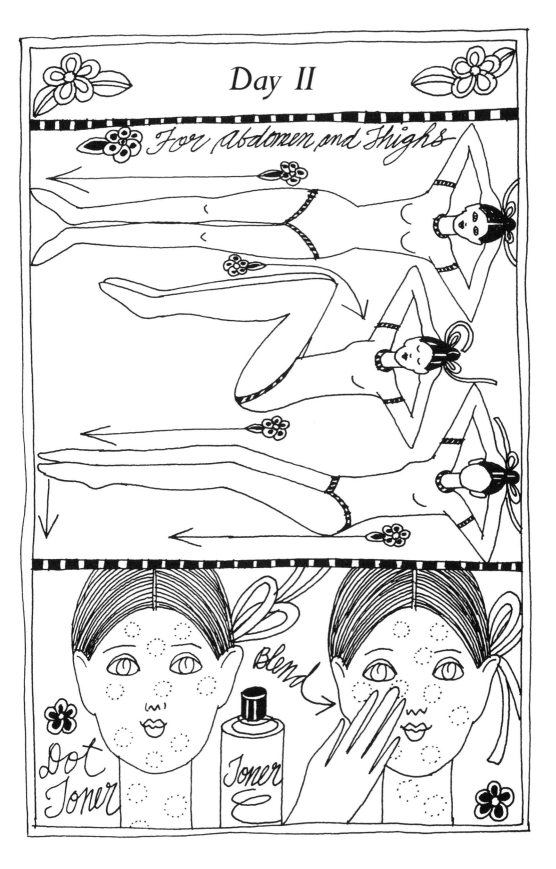

For abdomen and Thighs

Dot Toner

Toner

Blend

Menu

Breakfast

> 1,000 units Vitamin C and 1 therapeutic multiple-vitamin capsule with minerals
>
> ½ or whole cold boiled lobster with lemon juice and pepper if desired.
>
> Tea or coffee

Lunch

> 1 or 2 slices smoked salmon
>
> 12 or 18 cold boiled shrimp with 2 tbs. Russian dressing

Dinner

> 3 anchovies on 1 medium pimento
>
> E.O.F.'s sautéed scallops
>
> 1 glass of white wine, if desired
>
> Tea or coffee

* Do not forget eight glasses of liquids!

E.O.F.'s Sautéed Scallops

24 bay scallops
½ cup white wine
¼ cup chopped shallots
¼ tsp. chopped garlic
¼ tsp. salt
2 tbs. margarine
¾ tsp. powdered fennel
3 tsp. Pernod

Wash scallops in cold water; drain in colander and pat dry with paper towels.

In heavy skillet over low heat, sauté chopped shallots, garlic, margarine, wine, salt, white pepper, fennel and Pernod. Cook very slowly about 30 minutes. Then add scallops and sauté about 8 minutes.

Exercise One / To Limber Up

Lie on stomach, arms extended in front of you and chin on floor. Lift legs together from floor slowly, inhaling as you do; lower slowly, exhaling as you do. Try to keep your chin on the floor as you do this exercise. Repeat this exercise 10 times and work up to 20.

Exercise Two / For Waist

Sit cross-legged on floor. Clasp hands behind head and inhale. Bend to right, exhaling as you do. When you have reached as far as you can go, hold position for 3 seconds. Slowly return to upright position, inhaling as you do. Now bend to the left, exhaling as you do, hold position for 3 seconds and slowly return to upright position, inhaling as you do. Repeat this exercise 10 times on each side; work up to 20.

Exercise Three | For Abdomen and Thighs

Lie on back, legs straight out on floor, hands clasped behind your head. Inhale as you bend knees and slowly draw them upward to your chest. Exhale as you stretch your legs straight out and slowly lower them to the floor. Repeat 10 times and work up to 20.

Exercise Four | For Back

Lie on stomach with your chin on floor, arms stretched in front of you. Keep your feet, toes down, on the floor and raise your arms and head, arching your back from the floor, inhaling as you do. Slowly lower your head and arms, exhaling. Repeat 10 times and work up to 20.

Exercise Five | For Arms

Stand erect. Extend arms straight out from sides. Breathing deeply in and out, make small circles to the front with both arms at the same time. Then reverse and make small circles to the rear. Do not go too fast or the movement will be jerky. Repeat 10 times in each direction. Work up to 20.

Exercise Six | For Circulation

Stand straight on floor. Now inhale and exhale as you pretend you are skipping rope. Lift your knees high as you rapidly skip the imaginary rope. Repeat 10 times and work up to 20.

Skin Tones Are Changeable

Can you imagine a girl with perfect features and skin not being a model because of a ruddy complexion? Do you think that the glamorous women of the world are defeated by fading suntans at the end of the season at the beach? Of course they're not. They are the feminine women, the sexy women, the alluring women of the world, and they know all the tricks. They know how to change their skin tones.

The trick for changing your skin tone is really so simple that it would be a shame to ignore it. There are at most of the beauty counters today skin toners. They come in many shades.

I have found that pale green is perfect for blocking out ruddy complexions and freckles. Lilac is just right for concealing sallow skin. Many other colors are available, but I feel these two are the most effective.

Skin toner is applied on top of the moisture. Dot it sparingly all over your face and blend. The effect is weird, but when you apply base on top you'll see that you've achieved the effect you desired. You'll have to throw away your old makeup, as skin toners block out color. You'll have to use one at least two shades darker than the base you had. You'll probably have to add color with one of those shiny clear color gels or sticks that give that extra glow to your complexion. You can experiment until you find what you want at beauty counters everywhere.

Now look at yourself again. That's part of the game of concentration. Do you like how you look? There's the new you beginning to shine through: soft, sexy, beautifully toned skin that's a big part of being a woman, a real woman—that's *you*.

Day III

For Legs

Right Leg

Left Leg

Eight glasses of liquids

Menu

Breakfast

> 1,000 units Vitamin C and 1 therapeutic multiple-vitamin capsule with minerals
> 1 or 2 slices smoked whitefish with ¼ lemon
> Tea or coffee

Lunch

> 1 or 2 cups clam broth (canned)
> Fresh crabmeat salad with either cocktail sauce or lemon juice and pepper (You may use canned or frozen crabmeat if the fish market does not have fresh crabmeat.)

Dinner

> 1 deviled egg
> Seafood Stew Roman style
> 1 glass of white wine, if desired

* Do not forget eight glasses of liquids!

Deviled Egg

1 egg, hard-boiled
1 tsp. Durkee's Famous Sauce
paprika

If the egg is refrigerated, place it gently in 3 cups of *cold* water; bring to a boil *slowly*. This is to avoid cracking the egg. Simmer for 20 minutes, remove from water and cool to room temperature. Then place the egg in refrigerator to chill. *Or:* If the egg is at room temperature, place it *gently* in *warm* water, and proceed as outlined above.

(Eggs should be cooked slowly; fast cooking toughens them.)

When egg is chilled, remove the shell carefully. Cut egg in half lengthwise, and place the yolk from each half into a small bowl. Mash the yolk with a fork, add the Durkee's Famous Sauce and blend gently.

Fill each half of the egg white with the yolk mixture; sprinkle tops with a "shake" of paprika. Cover loosely (cover should not touch the deviled egg); chill in refrigerator, but serve as soon as possible.

Seafood Stew Roman Style

½ clove garlic, chopped

pinch red pepper

½ onion, chopped

2 tbs. salad oil

⅛ squid, skinned, cleaned and cut in small pieces
(Can omit—it will not change the recipe in any
way.)

¼ cup dry white wine

1 tsp. tomato paste

1 cup water

salt to taste

¼-lb. cod fillet

⅛ lb. shrimp, chilled, deveined and chopped

⅛ lb. scallops, cut in small pieces

⅛ lb. halibut, cut in small pieces

In a medium-size saucepan, sauté the garlic, the red pepper and the onions in the salad oil until the onions are delicately colored. Add water and bring to a boil. Add the squid, cover and cook over a *low* flame for 30 minutes, or until the squid is tender. Add the wine and cook at high boil for 15 minutes. Add the tomato paste, and cook for 5 minutes. Add the cod, shrimp, scallops and halibut and cook for 15 minutes longer.

Exercise One / To Limber Up

Lie on your stomach, arms extended in front of you, palms on floor. Inhaling deeply, simultaneously raise your right arm and left leg. Exhale as you lower to the floor. Reverse and raise left arm and right leg at the same time. Repeat 10 times with each arm.

Exercise Two / For Waist

Stand straight, hands on hips; inhale. Bend forward at the waist, lowering head as far as possible toward your toes and exhaling as you do. Inhale as you return to upright position. Repeat 10 times and work up to 20.

Exercise Three / For Legs

Lie on your back on floor, legs extended, hands clasped under head. Inhale as you slowly raise your right leg. Exhale as you slowly lower it. Repeat with left leg. Do this exercise 10 times with each leg.

Exercise Four | For Abdomen

Lie on back on floor. Place hands beneath buttocks. Spread your legs wide apart. Inhale as you slowly lift your legs three-quarters of the way up. Hold for a count of 3 and exhale as you slowly return your outstretched legs to floor. Start with 5 and work up to 20 times. If three-quarters of the way is too far, lift your legs only as far as is comfortable.

Exercise Five | For Calves and Thighs

Stand erect, feet about three inches apart, toes pointing straight ahead, hands on hips. Inhale. Sink into deep knee bend, exhaling as you do. Do not raise your heels from the floor. Inhale as you return to standing position. I'll be surprised if you can get down more than a few inches at first. Just keep plugging away and you'll get farther down each time. Start with 10 times and work up to 20.

Exercise Six | For Circulation

Stand erect, hands on hips. Raise yourself to the balls of your feet, keeping feet together. Jump forward about six inches; then jump back about six inches to where you started from. Jump forward again and repeat the sequence 10 times in each direction, breathing in and out deeply as you jump backward and forward. Work up to 20 times.

There's Nothing Pretty About False Teeth

Chances are you're starting to feel a little bit better about yourself today, because you know that soon you're going to look in the mirror and like what you see all over. But suppose you get your figure and face in perfect shape and suddenly you start to lose your teeth? A natural thing in the course of time? No! Not at all. And there's nothing pretty about a set of dentures in a glass beside the bed. It's a real romance killer.

Bleeding gums mean that you may be losing your teeth. Do you know how I found out? I lost some of mine. Perfectly good, sound, cavity-free teeth—and only my annual visit to the Strang Clinic saved me from losing more.

Every year I go to the Strang Clinic for a checkup. It's a very thorough checkup, and some years ago the doctor told me that my gums were in very poor shape. She advised my going to a periodontist.

"What's a periodontist?" I inquired. "A periodontist is a dentist whose only concern is care of the gums" was the answer. Well, I looked in the mirror and my teeth looked just fine. I went to a periodontist, who took X rays—and who recommended extensive dental work because of my gums. But I had no cavities and therefore did nothing.

I will not belabor you with a detailed account of what happened. Suffice it to say that I lost two perfectly sound white teeth as a result of ignoring professional advice. Today I know that more people lose their teeth to gum disease than to decay.

To prevent losing your teeth, start taking care of your gums before it's too late. Start your entire family on a program of gum care that will keep all your teeth healthy and brighten your smiles for all the years to come.

Every day after *both* breakfast and dinner you must follow this program:

1. Take dental floss or tape and work it up and down in each space between teeth.

2. Buy a rubber gum stimulator or use a toothbrush that has one at the end. Place the tip in each space between teeth and work it up and down ten times.

3. Use a water pick in each space between teeth.

4. Brush upper teeth downward and lower teeth upward—outer and inner surfaces both—making sure that you concentrate on the gums in order to exercise them.

Time-consuming? You bet it is! Tooth-saving? Guaranteed! Remember who and what you are becoming; your teeth are part of the totally feminine you!

Day IV

Menu

Breakfast

> 1,000 units of Vitamin C and 1 therapeutic multiple-vitamin capsule with minerals
> 1 or 2 slices of smoked sturgeon
> Tea or coffee

Lunch

> Antipasto—2 sardines, 4 anchovies, 4 clams, small pimento, 2 black olives, 1 green olive, 1 or 2 large pieces of water-packed tunafish

Dinner

> Shrimp cocktail (6 large size with bottled cocktail sauce)
> Lobster Sheldon Tannen
> 1 glass of white wine, if desired

* Do not forget eight glasses of liquids!

Lobster Sheldon Tannen

1 medium-size live or frozen lobster
any inexpensive white wine to cover the lobster
2 sprigs tarragon
½ tbs. margarine
1 tsp. flour
salt and pepper (white) to taste
1 tsp. finely chopped chervil
1 tsp. finely chopped tarragon leaves
⅔ tbs. Pernod

Place the lobster in a deep pan and cover with the white wine. Add 2 sprigs of tarragon, but no other seasoning. Slowly and carefully bring wine to a boil and let the lobster simmer covered for 20 minutes.

Cool the wine and when lukewarm remove the lobster from the pan and cut the tail in sections about 1½ inches long. Split shells in half and crack the claws. Discard the black vein running from head to tail, and the small sac back of the head.

From the shells remove the green tomalley (liver) and the coral (if any). Put them in a small saucepan, and add ½ the margarine and the flour. Heat the mixture gently, blending into a smooth paste; gradually add enough of wine in which lobster was cooked to make a smooth sauce, the consistency of light cream. Season lightly with salt and white pepper to taste. When the sauce is smooth, blend in chervil and chopped tarragon leaves.

Place lobster pieces in a small casserole; add the rest of the margarine, cover and reheat gently.

When the margarine is bubbling, pour over the lobster, then add the slightly heated Pernod. Set aflame; when it has burned out, add the sauce. Turn the lobster pieces with a spoon so that the sauce covers each piece completely.

Cover the casserole and set it in a 250° oven for 15 minutes; this allows the lobster to absorb the flavors. Serve lobster in the casserole, sprinkled with chopped tarragon.

I've had this dish at Café Chauveron and L'Armorique in New York City. I'm not sure if this is the way they make it. My final advice came from Sheldon Tannen of the world-famous restaurant "21," and, as you will see, it's spectacular.

Exercise One / To Limber Up

Lie on your stomach with chin resting on the floor, your arms extended in front of you and your toes pointing to the rear. Holding arms together and legs together, raise them simultaneously from the floor, inhaling deeply as you do. Lower to floor and exhale. Do not be discouraged if you cannot raise your arms and legs more than a millimeter at first. Time will give your back muscles the strength they need. Start slowly with this exercise. Try it 3 times at first and eventually work up to 20.

Exercise Two / For Waist

Stand straight, feet together, hands on hips, stomach muscles taut. Snap hips forward and exhale. Snap hips to the right and inhale. Snap hips to the rear and exhale. Snap hips to the left and inhale. Snap hips back to starting position. Reverse the cycle by snapping hips forward, left, back and right. Repeat 20 times. This exercise resembles the motions of a stiff-jointed belly dancer.

Exercise Three / For Legs

Stand with feet together. Slowly raise right leg and bend your knee. Clasp your hands around your leg and pull it as close as possible to your chest. Inhale deeply as you do this; exhale slowly as you return to starting position. Repeat with each leg 10 times.

Exercise Four / For Abdomen

Lie on your right side with the right arm extended, keeping your head on arm. Balance yourself by placing your left hand on the floor at chest level. Inhale, and as you do try to lift both legs from the floor. Exhale as you return legs to the floor. Repeat on each side 10 times. Work up to 20.

Exercise Five / For Back and Arms

Stand straight. Bend from waist, fingers pointing toward floor. Make a fist with each hand, facing in. Bending elbows, bring your hands up to your chest. Try to exert a force as if you were lifting weights. Return to starting position. Breathe sharply as you do this exercise. Repeat 10 times.

Exercise Six / For Circulation

Stand with feet together. Extend left leg $2\frac{1}{2}$ feet and turn left foot at right angle to body. Place hands on hips, rise to balls of your feet and bounce, inhaling and exhaling sharply as you do. Repeat 10 times, then switch feet and repeat 10 times. Work up to 20.

There's More to Breathing Than Staying Alive

When you're being embraced by the light of your life, is it just a hug because he's home and nothing more? If that's what it has come to, it's time to change. I've learned a lot traveling around Europe, and foremost among the things I've learned is that European women are genuinely sexy! They really put us to shame.

Just for instance, you and I breathe. We breathe to stay alive. The European woman breathes to keep romance alive. She whispers in his ear, blows in his ear while dancing and talks with her chin on her hand and her mouth very close to his—and it's great!

Men really respond to this kind of treatment, and if you don't try to keep your romance alive in various little ways, then it dies. You both get bored, and that's bad.

Now, don't go leaping at the man in your life all at once. Maybe you can just sit on the arm of his chair when he's reading the paper and give him a kiss on the ear, or when he comes in the door, hug him and blow gently in his ear and then kiss him. Not just a peck—kiss him as if you mean it. It isn't the only answer, but it's a start on the way back to romance.

If you're going to take my advice (and you should), consider the problem these loving gestures bring up. What about your breath? If you do follow these European man-baiting techniques, will he recoil because of your breath? It could and does happen every day.

Bad breath is caused by a variety of things—upset stomach, bad teeth, bad gums—but the most common cause of bad breath is what you eat. Garlic, onions and horseradish definitely cause unpleasing breath odor.

When food is chewed, swallowed and digested, it is absorbed into the bloodstream. The blood in turn passes through the lungs, which then expel impurities as you breathe. If you have eaten something that will cause bad breath, this is how it will happen to you.

You can counteract bad breath by putting three drops of oil of peppermint into a cup of tea and drinking it. It's a nice thing to do at the end of the day. Breath sprays are effective too. But the best care of all is to be careful about what you eat and never eat garlic or onions unless you both eat them.

If you embark on the program of romance building, don't do it once and expect it all to happen. It's like exercise: the more you do, the better it gets.

Day V

Menu

Breakfast

> 1,000 units of Vitamin C and 1 therapeutic multiple-vitamin capsule with minerals
>
> 1 or 2 slices smoked salmon

Lunch

> Clam soup Iris Ory

Dinner

> 1 slice of sturgeon
>
> Poached chopped salmon wrapped in filet of sole with white wine
>
> 1 glass of white wine, if desired

* Do not forget eight glasses of liquids!

Clam Soup Iris Ory

10 littleneck clams
1 tbs. salad oil
¼ clove garlic
½ anchovy fillet, chopped
2 tsp. chopped parsley
⅛ tsp. oregano
½ cup red wine
½ cup warm water
1 tsp. tomato paste
⅛ tsp. salt
⅛ tsp. freshly ground black pepper

Scrub the clams thoroughly. Place the oil in a heavy medium-size saucepan; add the garlic and brown. Remove the garlic. Add the anchovy, the parsley, the oregano and the wine to the oil and cook 5 minutes. Add the tomato paste, the salt and the pepper and cook 5 minutes. Add the clams; add the water, cover the pan tightly and simmer until all the shells are open—about 5 minutes.

Poached Chopped Salmon Wrapped In Filet of Sole with White Wine

Court Bouillon

> 1½ cups water
> 6 tbs. dry white wine
> ⅔ tbs. wine vinegar
> ½ onion, thickly sliced
> ⅓ carrot, cut in 1-inch chunks
> ⅔ celery stalk, with leaves, cut in 1-inch chunks
> 1 sprig parsley
> ⅓ bay leaf
> pinch dried tarragon
> ¼ tsp. finely chopped fresh thyme or pinch of dried thyme
> 1 tsp. salt
> 2 peppercorns

In a 2-quart pot, bring all the ingredients for the court bouillon to a boil over high heat. Cover the pot, reduce the heat and simmer for 30 minutes. Strain through a fine sieve into a small, deep covered pan; set aside to cool until lukewarm. You can freeze the court bouillon and reuse.

     1 large piece of filet of sole
     4 oz. salmon (chopped)
     court bouillon
     parsley to garnish

Now, wash the fish in cold water; dry with paper towels. Roll the chopped salmon in the slice of sole and fasten the sole around the salmon with toothpicks (my fish market does this for me). Place the fish on a low rack in a small pan and add court bouillon to cover the fish by 1½ to 2 inches; add water if necessary. Cover the pan and slowly bring to a simmer; immediately reduce heat and cook, barely at a simmer, for 15 minutes. Carefully lift the fish from the court bouillon to a heated plate. Before serving, garnish with parsley sprigs.

Exercise One / To Limber Up

Sit with legs straight in front of you. Pull right foot in so that the sole of your right foot is touching the inside of your left leg. Draw up your left leg with sole flat on floor. Clasp your left leg over your right knee and place it on the floor. Hold your left ankle with your right hand and place your left hand on the floor behind you. Slowly inhale as you turn your head as far to the left as possible (keep body erect) and hold it there for the count of 3. Exhale as you return to center position, still holding ankle. Repeat 3 times; then repeat all movements on the opposite side.

Exercise Two / For Back

Assume kneeling position. Touch your forehead to the floor and extend your arms in back of you, clasping your hands behind your back. Raise your body until it is parallel to the floor and you are looking straight ahead, inhaling as you do. Hold for a count of 3. Exhale, and return to starting position. Repeat 10 times and work up to 20.

Exercise Three | For Upper Thighs (rear)

Lie on back with legs extended. Bend right leg, bringing foot as close to your bottom as possible. Raise foot slightly from floor and grasp the knee with both hands. Inhale and pull your knee as close to your chest as possible as you exhale. Then extend your leg and lower slowly to the floor. Repeat 10 times with your right leg and then 10 times with your left.

Exercise Four | For Waist

Lie on your right side with your head resting on your outstretched right arm. Place your left hand flat on the floor in front of you for support. Inhaling deeply, raise your legs, head, and chest from the floor; exhale slowly as you return. Then reverse the position. Repeat 10 times on each side.

Exercise Five | For Upper Thighs (front)

Kneel on floor, keeping body erect. Raise body from knees up and spread feet apart, toes pointing out in back of you. Slowly let your bottom sink to the floor between your feet. Hold for a count of 3, then raise your body up to your knees. Inhale as you raise your body, exhale as you sink to the floor. Start with 5 repetitions and increase to 20.

Exercise Six | For Circulation

Stand with your feet together, hands on hips. Rise to balls of your feet and jump to stride position, remaining on balls of your feet. Inhaling and exhaling sharply, jump back to closed foot position, still remaining on balls of feet. Start with 10 and work up to 20 times.

There's More to Your Mouth

Yesterday, I was telling you about watching European women breathe at their men. They do lots more with their mouths than that.

In the first place, there's the trick of making the mouth look sexy by makeup. This is part of the total picture of you. In *Eileen Ford's Book of Model Beauty*, I tell you how to apply basic lip makeup. But in this rehabilitation program you've got to know that and more! A voluptuous mouth is a mouth that is carefully and definitely outlined with a brush or pencil—the outline must be darker than the lip color. If your lips are thin, be sure to powder your lips first and go slightly above the outline. If your lips are full, go ever so slightly *under* your own lip line. Now fill in with lipstick. Check with whomever you're trying to please to see which shades of lipstick he likes on you. Then take a brush and paint gloss over your lips. The lips have little or no oil or moisture in them and have a tendency to look or be dry. The gloss that you apply is not only beneficial—it's what gives that sensuous look to the lips.

Look in the mirror, say the word "True," hold the position with your lips. That's the look of the women I've been telling you about. Don't be afraid to practice a few tempting movements of your lips. You'll find they become natural to you—and the reaction to those lips is going to be spontaneous combustion.

Menu

Breakfast

> 1,000 units Vitamin C and 1 therapeutic multiple-vitamin capsule with minerals
> 8 cold boiled shrimp

Lunch

> 1 cold Alaskan or Dungeness crab (fresh, frozen or canned) with mustard mayonnaise (Add any hot mustard to commercial mayonnaise to taste.)

Dinner

> 3 sardines with a squeeze of lemon and pepper
> Bouillabaisse
> 1 glass of white wine, if desired

* Do not forget eight glasses of liquids!

Bouillabaisse

Court Bouillon
> ¼ cup thinly sliced onion
> ⅛ cup thinly sliced leeks
> 4 tsp. salad oil
> ¾ cup water
> ¼ cup dry white wine
> ¼ lb. fish heads, bones and trimmings
> 1 ripe medium tomato, coarsely chopped
> pinch of crushed dried fennel seeds
> ⅛ tsp. finely chopped garlic
> 1¼ tsp. chopped parsley
> 1 bay leaf
> pinch of crushed saffron threads
> salt
> freshly ground pepper

Cook onions and leeks in oil over low heat, stirring frequently, for 5 minutes or until they are tender. Do not allow them to brown. (Onions may be substituted for the leeks.) Add water, wine, fish, tomato and herbs and cook uncovered over moderate heat for 30 minutes.

1-lb. live lobster, cut up and cracked

¼ lb. each of 3 kinds of firm, white fish: halibut, bass,
   haddock

¼ lb. live mussels (optional)

¼ lb. fresh or frozen sea scallops

½ cup Pernod

When the court bouillon is done, strain it through a fine sieve into a soup pot, pressing down hard on fish trimmings and vegetables with the back of a spoon to extract all the flavor. Then throw them away. Add Pernod and bring the strained stock to a boil over high heat. Add the lobster. Boil for 5 minutes; then lower the heat and add the fish and cook another 5 minutes. Finally, add the mussels (if you have them) and scallops and boil 5 minutes longer. Taste for seasoning.

Pour the soup into a bowl. Add the fish and seafood. Stir some rouille (recipe follows) into the soup. Normally bouillabaisse is served with French bread sliced and fried in garlic-flavored salad oil, then drained and covered with aioli—garlic-flavored mayonnaise, known as the butter of the Mediterranean. The bread is not for dieters, but we can enjoy the aioli (recipe follows, page 82).

Rouille

1 small green pepper, seeded and cut into small squares
½ tsp. dry chili pepper
1½ cups water
1 canned pimento, drained and dried
2 garlic cloves, coarsely chopped
2 tsp. salad oil

Simmer the green pepper and chili pepper in the water until tender (about 2 minutes). Remove from water and dry them with a paper towel. Combine simmered chili and pepper, pimento, garlic and salad oil in an electric blender. Blend at low speed until smooth, adding more oil if blender clogs. Transfer the sauce to a bowl. (Some people stir in enough bread crumbs to make it thick enough to hold its shape in a spoon; I don't.) Taste and season with chili peppers if necessary. It should be hot. Then stir the rouille into the bouillabaisse for flavor.

Aioli

This recipe is for much more aioli than you will need. Make it and store it in the refrigerator; you can use it with other things.

> 4 egg yolks
> 3 garlic cloves, chopped fine
> pinch salt
> pinch white pepper
> ¾ cup salad oil

With an eggbeater, beat the three egg yolks and garlic to a paste. Add the seasonings. Now add the oil a drop at a time (I use an electric hand beater at this point). When the oil is all beaten into the egg yolks, the mixture will look like thick mayonnaise—which it is. Stir it into the soup.

Exercise One | To Limber Up

Stand erect, feet about twelve inches apart. Clasp hands below your back. Raise your clasped hands behind your back until you feel a pull in your shoulder blades. Now bend back from the waist, allowing head to drop as far back as possible. Keep clasped hands as high as you can. Inhale very slowly. Exhale as you bend forward from the waist, raising your hands as high as possible behind you. Come up very slowly, inhaling as you do. Relax and repeat 5 times.

Exercise Two | For Waist

Kneel on left knee and stretch right leg to side for balance. Clasp hands above your head. Inhale. Exhale as you bend to the right until you feel stretch in your thigh. Do not overextend. Return to starting position, inhaling as you do. Repeat this exercise 10 times to the right. Then switch—placing your right knee on the floor, extending your left leg and leaning to the left as you exhale—and repeat 10 times.

Exercise Three / For Inner Upper Thighs

Lie on your right side with the right arm extended. Lift left leg as high as possible, inhaling. Lower slowly and exhale. Repeat 10 times on each side.

Exercise Four / For Abdomen

Lie on back, arms over head. Inhaling slowly, contract stomach muscles. Start with low muscles and gradually work up until muscles are tightened all the way to top of diaphragm. Hold for a count of 3. Exhale slowly, releasing muscles from diaphragm on down. Repeat 10 times; work up to 20.

Exercise Five / For Waist

Stand straight, feet together. Raise right arm over head, palm facing forward, inhaling as you do. Now bend forward and raise your left leg up and straight out, lowering your right arm until your fingers touch your left toes, exhaling as you do. Inhale as you return to starting position. Repeat 5 times and work up to 20. Repeat with opposite arm and leg.

Exercise Six / For Circulation

Run in place, kicking heels up as close as possible to your bottom. Breathe sharply in and out as you do this exercise. Repeat 10 times; work up to 20.

Voices Can Be Fascinating Too!

What comes out of that beautifully formed mouth of yours can be a variety of things. Conversation and voice are a part of the fascinating woman you're about to become. Is your voice appealing, mellow, low-pitched? If you don't know, go to an appliance store and pretend you're going to buy a tape recorder Speak into it and listen carefully to the sound that comes back. Like what you hear? If not, read on, because it's not hard to change a flat, monotonous or shrill voice into a voice that flows like velvet caressing the skin.

When I first went out to speak in public, I went to a speech coach, Betty Cashman. Betty put what I thought was my mellifluous voice on tape, and to my horror, I found it to be monotonous to a point that surprised me. I still go to Betty whenever I have to speak in public or do a commercial, and she gave me the following tips for you.

In the first place, you've got to think constantly about keeping your voice low and mellow. Call Information and ask for numbers—of anyone, real or imaginary. Keep your hand on your chest and try to make the sound come from there.

Keep the hand on your chest and say the letters of the alphabet.

Carefully articulate the beginning and end of every word.

Concentrate on it. When you're in the store, at the market, in a taxi, with people you don't know, practice; think low, think mellow, think pronunciation. You'll notice that some letters in this paragraph are underlined. Read them aloud. Practice by saying the days of the week, then the months of the year. Listen to the poor enunciation around you. Decide for yourself today what kind of woman you are going to be. A shrill shrew with a voice that grates, or a true sophisticate with a voice and a way of speaking that can captivate? It's yours for the doing.

Menu

Breakfast

      1,000 units of Vitamin C and 1 therapeutic multiple-
          vitamin capsule with minerals
      ½ cold lobster (boiled, average size)

Lunch

      2 artichoke bottoms with crabmeat

Dinner

      Ermine Ford's New Orleans Shrimp Gumbo
      1 glass of white wine, if desired

* Do not forget eight glasses of liquids!

Artichoke Bottoms with Crabmeat

2 artichoke bottoms (canned)
4 oz. crabmeat
1 tsp. chopped onion
1 tsp. capers
1 tsp. homemade mayonnaise (recipe follows)
4 medium-size lettuce leaves

Combine the crabmeat, onion, capers and mayonnaise. Wash and dry lettuce and arrange on a salad plate. Place artichoke bottoms in center of plate and arrange the crabmeat mixture on top of them. Serve cold.

Mayonnaise

2 egg yolks
½ tsp. dry mustard
1 level tsp. salt
⅛ tsp. cayenne pepper
½ tsp. lemon juice
1 tsp. tarragon vinegar
¼ cup vegetable oil

Beat the egg yolks, seasonings, lemon juice and vinegar with a mixer until light and fluffy. Very slowly add the vegetable oil, drop by drop at first, beating all the time. As the oil begins to "take" and the mayonnaise thickens, pour more quickly. This mayonnaise will keep well in a screw-top jar in the refrigerator.

Ermine Ford's New Orleans Shrimp Gumbo

2 tsp. margarine
1⅓ tbs. chopped onion
1 tsp. chopped green pepper
¾ tbs. diced celery
4 tbs. okra (fresh, frozen or canned)
3 tbs. tomatoes (canned, solid pack)
½ tsp. chopped parsley
pinch of crumbled bay leaf
5½ tbs. chicken stock (canned)
salt, pepper
12 shrimp
½ cup crabmeat (optional)

Melt 1 tsp. margarine in a medium skillet. Add chopped onion, green pepper and diced celery, and cook until tender. Wash the okra until not slimy. Add the okra, tomatoes, parsley, bay leaf and chicken stock. Salt and pepper to taste. Cook until vegetables are tender but not overdone.

When the vegetables are well cooked, add the raw shrimp. When the shrimp are cooked, add the crabmeat, if used. Cook together until everything is thoroughly heated. Serve in soup bowls.

My husband adds Tabasco sauce to the dish. Everyone down South eats it with rice. We do not. If you have guests, they can.

Exercise One / To Limber Up

Kneel on floor, body erect. Stretch your arms in front of you. Lower your hands to the floor, with your head between your arms. Keep your bottom up and back curved. Exhale as you slowly slide your hands forward. Return to starting position, inhaling as you do. This exercise must be done very slowly 10 times.

Exercise Two / For Waist

Stand with legs apart. Inhale deeply as you raise your arms above your head, palms facing inward. Exhale as you bend from waist, fingertips reaching for the floor, about two inches in front of your feet. In rapid succession, bounce your body so that fingers touch three inches in back of where you first touched and finally touch the floor directly behind your heels. In other words, you bounce so that your fingers are first in front of your toes, second in the middle of your feet, then between your heels. Inhale as you slowly return to arms-overhead position. Repeat 10 times; work up to 20.

Exercise Three / For Thighs (back)

Sit on floor, legs extended in front of you, hands clasped behind head. Inhale as you slowly pull knees to chest, raising your feet from the floor. Straighten legs in front of you, exhale and lower as slowly as possible. Work up to 20 times.

Exercise Four / For Inner Thighs

Lie on back on floor. Raise legs straight up. Inhale. Exhale as you spread legs apart slowly to the side and inhale as you pull them slowly together. Repeat 10 times and work up to 20.

Exercise Five / For Back

Stand straight, feet together. Bend your left knee and raise your left foot in back of you until you can grasp your left ankle with your left hand. Inhaling slowly, raise your right arm above your head with palm facing forward. Slowly arch back slightly, head and neck relaxed. Hold position for 3 seconds. Exhale as you return to starting position. Repeat on opposite foot. The ideal performance of this exercise would be to hold the extended position for at least 1 minute.

Exercise Six / For Circulation

Grasp your left knee in front of you and hop on your right foot. Hop 10 times. Then switch and hop on your left foot 10 times holding your right knee. Work up to 20 times.

Eyes Are for More than Looking

Since the days of Nefertiti, women have been using eye makeup to enhance their natural beauty, and there are probably few modern women who don't realize the advantage of some strategically placed eye shadow, eye liner and mascara. It's a subject I covered very thoroughly in *Eileen Ford's Book of Model Beauty*.

However, in thinking about how alluring women use their eyes to convey a thousand hidden messages, I realized that there's something very few women know. Professional beauties all over the world use false eyelashes. Eyelashes so cunningly applied that no one knows they are not their very own.

Imagine sitting next to or across from someone—sipping your iced tea and looking deep into his eyes, slowly lowering your lashes, then looking back into the very depths of his eyes. Even if he's been around for twenty or thirty years, it's not too late to learn to flirt all over again.

When I decided that what I needed was false eyelashes, I decided that strip eyelashes weren't for me, as I was allergic even to surgical adhesive and they made my eyes red. So I went to Jean Kane of New York's Eyelash Studio and asked for help. Miss Kane has taught many of our models and applies individual eyelashes to many of the world's outstanding beauties. She teaches our models as I will now teach you.

You may buy individual lashes or take an inexpensive pair of strip lashes and pull the single lash from the end of the strip with a tweezer. If you are using a strip, trim the lashes first with a single-edge razor blade. Place the lashes on a sheet of white paper. Put a mirror flat on a table so that you will be looking down into it. Pick up each eyelash in turn with tweezer and touch it to eyelash glue so that you have a very small amount of glue on the lash. Attach the lash about halfway back on the underside of one of your own lashes. You can trim the lengths with blunt-end scissors (such as nose-hair trimmers). Do not cut straight across, but cut the lashes at uneven lengths for a feathered look.

I keep my eyelashes on for days if it isn't windy, washing around them carefully. If a few fall out, I replace them. When the eyelashes finally become stiff and unnatural-looking, I take them off by pressing a hot washcloth to my lashes and gently pulling off the lashes as they come loose.

When you've mastered this trick, use those eyes of yours for what they were meant for.

Again you'll find the mirror a great help. Practice various expressions from innocent to sexy, from sad to gay, and try to use them every time you look at someone. Stare deep into his eyes, smile with your eyes, let your eyes smoulder.

Where did romance go? You'll find it never left at all.

Second Week

. . . You're on Your Way

Fill this in; you'll see a little progress.

WEIGHT	BUST	WAIST	HIPS	THIGHS

Day VIII

Menu

Breakfast

> 1,000 units of Vitamin C and 1 therapeutic multiple-
> vitamin capsule with minerals
> Cold crabmeat (4 oz.)

Lunch

> Jerry Ford's Seafood Chef's Salad

Dinner

> Baked clams Casino
> Poached bass with white margarine sauce
> 1 glass of white wine, if desired

* Do not forget eight glasses of liquids!

Jerry Ford's Seafood Chef's Salad

2 oz. boiled lobster (fresh or canned)
4 cold boiled shrimp
2 oz. crabmeat (fresh or canned)
½ cup celery, diced small
1 tsp. grated onion
3 tbs. vinegar-and-oil dressing
4 medium-size lettuce leaves

Combine lobster, shrimp, crabmeat; add celery, onion and dressing. Mix well. Arrange lettuce leaves on plate and arrange salad on lettuce.

Clams Casino

½ dozen cherrystone clams
1 tbs. margarine
1 tbs. finely chopped green pepper
1 tbs. finely chopped onion
2 pieces raw bacon

Have the fish market open the clams. Remove the clams and in the bottom of each shell place a small piece of margarine. Place the clams on top of the margarine and put the shells on a layer of rock salt in a shallow tin baking pan. Top each clam with a pinch each of finely chopped green pepper and onion. Cover with a piece of raw bacon the size of the clam.

Broil 3 inches from the flame for 6 to 8 minutes, turning the bacon once to broil it on both sides. Serve the clams in the shells, and make sure they are very hot.

Poached Bass with White Margarine Sauce

Court Bouillon

        1½ cups water

        6 tbs. dry white wine

        ⅔ tbs. wine vinegar

        ½ onion, thickly sliced

        ⅓ carrot, cut in 1-inch chunks

        ⅔ stalk celery, with leaves, cut in 1-inch chunks

        1 sprig parsley

        ⅓ bay leaf

        ⅙ tsp. finely cut fresh tarragon *or* a pinch of dried tarragon

        ⅙ tsp. finely cut fresh thyme *or* a pinch of dried thyme

        1 tsp. salt

        2 peppercorns

In a 2-quart pot, place all the ingredients for the court bouillon and bring to a boil. Partially cover the pot, reduce heat and simmer for 30 minutes. Strain through a fine sieve into a small, deep roasting pan that has a cover. Allow to cool until lukewarm.

¾ lb. bass, boned
> (any fish with firm white meat, such as red snap-
> per, haddock, cod, pollack, rockfish or lake trout,
> may be substituted.)

Wash the fish in cold water; dry with paper towels. Place in a roasting pan (on a low rack is possible) and add court bouillon to cover the fish by 1½ to 2 inches; add water if necessary. Cover the pan and bring to a slow simmer; immediately reduce heat and cook, barely at a simmer, for 15 minutes. Remove the pan from heat and leave fish in it (covered) for another 15 minutes. Carefully lift the fish to a heated plate. Serve with white margarine sauce (recipe follows) and parsley sprigs.

White Margarine Sauce

4 tbs. of liquid in which fish was cooked
2 shallots, finely chopped
¼ cup tarragon wine vinegar
2 tsp. salt
white pepper
¼ cup margarine

Combine fish liquid, shallot, vinegar, salt and pepper in a small pan and simmer slowly until about ⅛ cup remains. Pour the mixture into the top of a double boiler. When the water under the double boiler comes to a boil, start adding the margarine a bit at a time, beating constantly with a wire whisk. When the sauce is well blended and sort of foamy, it is finished.

Exercise One / To Limber Up

Sit on floor, knees bent, and clasp toes with your hands. Inhale. Slowly walk your feet forward on the heels, exhaling as you do. Stop when your legs are extended as far as is comfortable. Still grasping toes with hands, walk your feet backward on heels, inhaling as you do, until body is erect. Repeat 10 times. Remember, your eventual aim is to touch your head to your knees with your legs fully extended. There is no rush; get there gradually.

Exercise Two / For Waist

Stand straight, feet together, hands on hips. Bend forward at the waist about one-third of the way down to your waist. Begin a slow circular motion to the left. Rotate body to the back, to the right and back to original position. When full circle is complete, reverse and circle from the right around to the left. Inhale and exhale slowly as you perform each circle. Do this exercise 10 times in each direction.

Exercise Three / For Thighs

Lie on floor, hands placed under your buttocks. Inhale and slowly raise your extended right leg. Exhale as you slowly lower it. Now inhale as you slowly raise left leg and exhale as you lower it. Repeat 10 times.

Exercise Four / For Calves and Thighs

Stand up straight. Grasp left foot in back of you with right hand. Extend left arm for balance. Inhale and slowly sink down on right leg. (You may hold on to the back of a chair as you do this. Do not go farther than is comfortable.) Inhale as you rise back up. Alternate 5 times on each leg. Work up to 20 times.

Exercise Five / For Back

Stand straight. Inhale as you look over your left shoulder. At the same time quickly lift your left leg straight in back of you. Exhale as you return to starting position. Now look over right shoulder and extend your right leg straight in back of you, again inhaling as you look back, exhaling as you return. Repeat 10 times. Again you may hold on to the back of a chair as you do this exercise.

Exercise Six / For Circulation

Stand with your feet together, arms at your sides. Jump to legs-apart position, landing squarely on both feet, and clap your hands above your head, inhaling sharply as you do. Jump back to original position, exhaling as you do. I call this the Jumping Jack. Repeat 20 times.

Use Your Eyebrows

If you're going to go all the way to becoming a more alluring you, then consider your eyebrows. Shaggy or too thin, too arched or not arched at all, the wrong eyebrow can undo all the good you've done with all the other tricks. Look at everyone else's eyebrows and you'll know what I'm saying is true. Women can slap on an awful lot of eye makeup and eyelashes and then forget that eyebrows are truly the frames for the eyes. The trick to having lovely brows is in the plucking, and here it is.

You will need:

1. Eyebrow brush
2. Hot face cloth
3. Tweezers
4. Ice cubes
5. An eyebrow pencil

The eyebrow begins directly above the inner corner of the eye.

The arch is directly above the outer edge of the iris when you look straight ahead.

The eyebrow ends at a point where a slim pencil slanted from the side of your nose past the outer corner of the eye meets the brow.

The beginning and end of the brow should be on the same level.

start with a hot face cloth

up *sideways* *tweeze*

Finish with ice cubes

1. Before tweezing, apply a hot face cloth to the brows. Using an eyebrow brush, brush them up and then sideways.

2. Tweeze them in the direction in which the hair grows. If it hurts, go over the area with an ice cube.

3. Pluck only one hair at a time.

4. Do not pluck hairs above the brow, except any strays at the end of the brow, or unless your brows are very bushy.

5. If you need to use an eyebrow pencil, use one that is one shade lighter than your hair. Brunettes use dark-brown pencil—never black; brownettes, from a medium-brown to a light-brown pencil. There are reddish pencils for redheads and a pale, almost grey-ish-silver pencil for blondes.

6. Use small, light strokes, as if you were drawing one hair at a time.

As the shade of your eyebrows should be one shade lighter than your hair, if you have had your hair lightened check the color of your brows. If it is too dark, lighten them with one of the facial-hair bleaches. When you have the bleach on the brows, check the color repeatedly—you don't want them too light; but should you bleach your brows too much, don't panic! They grow back in very quickly, and you can cover your mistake with a pencil.

After you've plucked your eyebrows into the correct shape, keep them plucked by checking every day or two. No lovely lady ever had extra hairs to spoil her lovely brows.

And remember to use your eyebrows. Lift them knowingly, significantly, and look warmly into his eyes. You'll see what I mean as your life takes on new dimensions.

Menu

Breakfast

> 1,000 units of Vitamin C and 1 therapeutic multiple-
> vitamin capsule with minerals
> 1 or 2 slices of smoked sturgeon

Lunch

> Clam broth (bottled)
> Nancy Otte's Crab Delight

Dinner

> 6 Oysters Rockefeller
> Shrimp Madras
> 1 glass of white wine, if desired

* Do not forget eight glasses of liquids!

Nancy Otte's Crab Delight

2 eggs
salt, pepper, thyme
pinch of tarragon
2 oz. crabmeat (fresh or canned)
½ tbs. finely chopped onion
1 medium green pepper, finely chopped
¾ tbs. finely chopped parsley
½ tbs. melted margarine
pinch of baking powder

Separate the yolks and whites of the eggs. Beat the yolks until light. Season with salt, pepper and pinch of tarragon (a good pinch). Add the crabmeat; mix carefully—don't mash the crabmeat to shreds.

Add the onion, green pepper and parsley to the crab; now add the melted margarine, and sprinkle the baking powder over the mixture. Mix well, but remember not to break up the crabmeat.

Beat the egg whites until stiff but not dry. Fold in gently. Make sure that everything is well blended, with nothing unmixed at the bottom of the bowl.

Preheat a 7- or 8-inch skillet or an omelet pan. Using a pastry brush, lightly cover the bottom of the pan with a film of margarine. Carefully place the crabmeat mixture in the hot skillet. Cook until brown on one side; turn carefully and brown on the other side. Be sure it is golden brown so that it turns freely.

Oysters Rockefeller

6 oysters on the half shell—prepared by the fish market

½ cup margarine

¼ cup chopped parsley

¼ cup chopped shallots or scallions

1 cup chopped watercress

¼ tsp. dried pulverized fennel seeds

2 tbs. Pernod

salt and freshly ground pepper to taste

Heat oven for 10 minutes at 450 degrees. Fill a tin pie plate with rock salt. Heat the margarine in a saucepan. Add watercress and fennel and cook for 2 minutes. Then pour the mixture into a blender with the rest of the ingredients and puree them. Put about one tablespoon of mixture on each oyster and place the oysters on the rock salt. Bake the oysters for about 5 minutes.

You may double recipe if you are hungry. It can't hurt, and they are good!

Shrimp Madras

12 medium-size shrimp (fresh)
⅛ tsp. dried mint
⅛ tsp. dried red pepper flakes
½ tsp. turmeric
⅛ tsp. ground coriander seeds
salt and pepper
¼ tsp. grated fresh ginger, or half this amount pow-
    dered
½ clove garlic, finely chopped
⅛ tsp. ground cumin
¼ medium-size onion
1 tbs. margarine
¼ cup yogurt (omit this if you like very hot curry)
¼ tsp. liquid chutney or ginger in syrup
½ tsp. chopped parsley or fresh coriander leaves
juice of ¼ lemon

Peel and devein the raw shrimp. Wash them in cold water
and dry. Place raw shrimp in a mixing bowl and add the mint,
red pepper, turmeric, ground coriander, salt and pepper to taste,

120

ginger, garlic and cumin. Mix well with the hands until all the shrimp are coated. Let stand an hour or so.

Peel onion and grate it on the coarse side of your kitchen grater. This is essential; chopped onion will not work as well.

Heat 1 tsp. margarine in a deep frying pan and add the onion, stirring. Cook until the onion is fairly dry, without browning. Do not let the onion stick to the skillet as it is liable to do.

Add the remaining margarine and the shrimp mixture. Cook, stirring and gently turning the shrimp in the pan, until the shrimp start to turn light red all over. Add the yogurt and liquid chutney. Simmer 10 minutes, covered.

Uncover and cook over moderately high heat 10 minutes longer. Add chopped parsley, lemon juice and salt and pepper to taste. Serve hot.

Exercise One / To Limber Up

Stand against wall (feet should be about twelve inches from the baseboard), arms folded across chest. Inhaling deeply, flatten back against the wall and sink down on knees to a position similar to sitting on a chair, contracting your abdomen as you do. Hold for a count of 3 and slowly exhale as you slide back up against wall to standing position. Repeat once and work up to 10 times.

Exercise Two / For Waist

Stand straight, feet apart, hands on hips. Inhale. Bend forward quickly as far as possible. Bounce twice from the waist, to a count of 1, 2; this is simply a double bounce. Return to starting position, inhaling as you do. This exercise should be done quickly and with vigor. Repeat 10 times and work up to 20.

Exercise Three / For Abdomen

Lie on floor, hands clasped behind head. While exhaling, slowly draw feet toward you across floor until knees are bent and feet are flat on the floor; at the same time swing body forward until elbows touch knees. Inhale as you slowly return to starting position. Repeat 10 times; work up to 20.

Exercise Four / For Legs

Lie on back on floor, hands under bottom. Lift legs straight in the air. Inhale and exhale as you slowly move your legs backward and forward: right leg forward, left leg back; left leg forward, right leg back. Repeat 10 times and work up to 20. Each pair of leg movements counts as 1.

Exercise Five / For Arms

Stand straight, feet astride. Extend arms straight out at sides, palms facing forward. Keep arms at shoulder level throughout exercise. To a count of 1, 2, snap your arms back. To the count of 3, 4, cross your hands in front of you—first right over left, then left over right. This should be done so that only the wrists overlap, not the arms. Inhale sharply on the 1, 2, then exhale; inhale again on 3, 4 and then exhale. Repeat 10 times.

Exercise Six | For Circulation

Stand straight. Hop on ball of left foot with left arm at side, swinging right foot and right arm out wide. Quickly switch to right leg and swing out left foot and left arm. Alternate quickly, breathing in and out sharply. The effect should be like that of a pendulum swinging back and forth. Start with 10 swings on each foot and work up to 20.

Frizzies Are Bad

I know that if you have straight hair you long for curly locks and if your hair is a mass of ringlets you long for straight hair. Either problem can be solved, by a permanent or straightening; the processes are similar and completely effective. But—suppose you have hair, curly or straight, that is just as you like it except in damp weather. What then? Should you be forced to face all humid days looking as if you'd been partially electrocuted? Is this the super creature we've been working to be? How can a radiant beauty peer out at the world through a frizzy hairdo? She can't; and she doesn't have to—because frizzy hair is a thing of the past if you treat it the models' way.

For equipment you'll need:

1. A brush
2. A comb
3. A hand hair dryer

Start by brushing your hair through until there's nary a snarl. Then take the comb and separate one section at a time. Hold the section straight out from your scalp.

Now take the preheated hair dryer and pass it from the roots down to the ends of the outstretched section of hair you are holding. This is in effect ironing your hair smooth. Do this as

125

much as is needed to drive the frizzies out of the hair. It's infallible.

Once you've got your hair under control you can use it as you will. Sometimes let it fall over your eye as you're talking earnestly; run your hands slowly, suggestively through it, be it long or short. Make your hair work for you; it's a very potent weapon in any woman's bag of tricks.

126

Day X

For The Waist

Menu

Breakfast

      1,000 units of Vitamin C and 1 therapeutic multiple-
        vitamin capsule with minerals

      1 or 2 slices smoked whitefish with lemon

Lunch

      1 or 2 slices cold striped bass with Sauce Gribiche
      (poached the night before and chilled)

Dinner

      Smoked trout—1 small whole, or freeze ½ for another
        day

      Positano Seafood Stew

      1 glass of white wine, if desired

* Do not forget eight glasses of liquids!

Sauce Gribiche

1 hard-boiled egg
¼ tsp. dry mustard
¼ cup salad oil
3 tsp. white-wine vinegar
¼ tsp. salt
dash cayenne pepper
3 tsp. chopped gherkins
1½ tbs. chopped capers
¾ tbs. chopped parsley
½ tsp. chopped chives
¼ tsp. dried tarragon

Make a mayonnaise: mash egg yolk with mustard until smooth; add oil very slowly, alternating with vinegar to taste. Season with salt and cayenne pepper. When all the oil has been added, mix in all remaining ingredients and the egg white, chopped up.

Positano Seafood Stew

1 live 1-pound lobster

1 tbs. salad oil

1½ tbs. finely chopped onion

¼ tsp. finely chopped garlic

pinch of crumbled dried sage leaves

½ cup white wine

1½ tbs. tomato paste, dissolved in 3 tbs. water

4 tsp. fresh or bottled clam broth

½ tsp. crumbled bay leaf

1 tsp. salt

2 oz. squid (optional) cut into ½-inch rings

2 oz. each of 2 kinds of firm, white fish (halibut, cod, flounder, mackerel, pollack, snapper, bass or rock-fish) cut into 2-inch serving pieces

2 oz. whole bay scallops, or sliced sea scallops

1 tsp. finely chopped fresh parsley

½ tsp. freshly grated lemon peel

Ask your fish market to prepare the live lobster as follows: Place the lobster on its back and slice off the whole tail section. Cut tail in half lengthwise down the center. Cut off large claws and crack them. Cut off the feelers and split the body section in half lengthwise. Remove and discard the gelatinous sac (or stomach) near the head, and the long intestine attached to it. Then remove and set aside the greenish-brown tomalley (or liver) and the black, caviarlike eggs (or coral) if any.

Heat the oil in heavy 2-quart saucepan (iron if possible). Add the onion, and cook it, stirring frequently, over moderate heat for 8 to 10 minutes until it is limp. Add the garlic and sage and cook, stirring, for 2 minutes longer. Pour in wine and boil briskly over high heat, stirring constantly, until mixture has been reduced to about $\frac{1}{8}$ cup; then add tomato-paste water, clam broth, bay leaf and salt. Reduce heat and simmer sauce, partially covered, for 10 minutes.

Add lobster; cover and cook another 5 minutes. Then place the fish in the sauce, cover the pan and cook for 5 minutes. Finally, add scallops and squid and cook, covered, for 5 minutes. With a large, slotted spoon carefully transfer the cooked fish and seafood to heated soup bowl. Press the tomalley and coral through a fine sieve and stir them into the hot sauce. Simmer for 3 minutes; taste for seasoning; then pour the sauce over fish and seafood. Sprinkle chopped parsley and grated lemon peel on top.

This is a lot of work for one person, but it's great. I suggest one guest the night you prepare it.

Exercise One | To Limber Up

Sit on floor. Extend right leg and draw your left leg into your groin. Inhale and raise arms till your fingers point to the sky. Slowly exhale and lower your body. With both hands, grasp whichever part of your right leg you can comfortably reach, be it knee, calf, ankle or foot. Hold for a count of 3. Return to starting position, inhaling as you do, and repeat entire exercise 10 times. Now reverse position, extending left leg and drawing right leg into groin, and repeat the exercise 10 times. Work up to 20 times on each side.

Exercise Two | For Waist

Stand straight, legs apart. Raise hands over head, inhale deeply, turn body from waist to the right. While exhaling, bend over and touch floor with your fingers to the right of the toes of your right foot. Bounce and touch fingers to floor behind the heel. Straighten up, inhaling as you do. Repeat to the left. Repeat 10 times on each side; work up to 20.

Exercise Three / For Inner Thighs

Sit on floor with your legs extended, hands in back of you. Lift one leg, inhale and hold for a count of 3. Return to starting position exhaling slowly. Alternate legs, 10 times each.

Exercise Four / For Abdomen

Lie on back on floor, hands under bottom. Inhale as you raise your legs straight about three inches from the floor. Keeping your feet together, make a little circle first to the right, then to the left. Exhale as you slowly lower legs to floor. Repeat 5 times and work up to 20. This is hard at first and may never be easy, but it's great.

Exercise Five / For Waist

Sit on floor, legs spread apart. Place hands on hips; inhale. Exhale as you bend forward and try to touch forehead to floor. Repeat 10 times and work up to 20. How long it will take you to get all the way down, I can't imagine. I am not there yet, but I keep on trying. It's fun!

133

Exercise Six / For Circulation

Stand on right leg holding left foot behind you with left hand. Hop 10 times on ball of foot, inhaling and exhaling sharply with each hop. Reverse; hop on the other foot 10 times. Work up to 20 times.

Drooping Locks, Drooping Romance

Nobody can look perfect all the time: that's a fact. Even if you've just come from the beauty salon or taken your hair out of curlers, a sudden gust of wind or a bit of rain can cause hair to droop here and there. Maybe you haven't set your hair at all and suddenly you've a date or a guest. Then what? Must it be disaster? Not if you own a set of electric curlers.

Models have to look as if their hair has just been set all the time. There is not a model who doesn't carry a set of electric curlers to work. Most studios have a set, too. But there's always the chance that instead of the studio the photographer may use a location such as an apartment or restaurant, and then the model will need her own curlers.

Most electric curlers have points on them, for goodness knows what reason, as the only cause these points on the rollers seem to serve is that of breaking the hair that's wound around them. Models get around this by filing the points off the rollers and then covering them with aluminum foil. If a model's hair should start to collapse during a session, it's only a matter of minutes until her hair looks as if it had been freshly set.

No two people know each other so well that you as a woman can appear in rollers in front of anyone. It's downright ugly and most unfeminine. How can anyone look at you and remember that first date? So keep your head full of curlers in the privacy of your room. Nevermore will you have to use the excuse "I didn't have time." Follow the models' way to a perfect set, and retain the mystery of your beautiful hair as your very own secret.

Day XI

Menu

Breakfast

    1,000 units of Vitamin C and 1 therapeutic multiple-
        vitamin capsule with minerals

    Cold crabmeat (4 oz.)

Lunch

    Cold seafood in Chimichurri sauce

Dinner

    3 love apples stuffed with tuna and onions

    Lobster French-American Style

    1 glass of white wine, if desired

* Do not forget eight glasses of liquids!

Chimichurri Sauce

⅛ cup lemon juice
¼ cup salad oil
½ cup chopped shallots
1 tbs. water
½ tsp. minced garlic
½ cup chopped parsley
¾ tsp. dried oregano
¼ tsp. chili pepper
¾ tsp. salt
¾ tsp. coarse-grained black pepper

Combine liquid ingredients in a bowl with a whisk. Then add the other ingredients. Allow sauce to stand overnight if possible.

6 cold boiled shrimp
⅛ lb. crabmeat
or any other plain cold leftover fish or seafood

Place seafood in a bowl. Pour sauce over seafood. Place mixture on 4 lettuce leaves and serve.

Love Apples Stuffed with Tuna and Onions

3 cherry tomatoes
1/4 cup cooked tunafish
1 tsp. chopped onion
1 tsp. mayonnaise
1/4 tbs. chopped parsley
pinch of salt
black pepper, freshly ground
pinch of cayenne
parsley sprigs
paprika (3 little dashes)

Scoop out tomatoes, leaving little hollow shells, which will be stuffed.

Combine tuna, chopped onion, mayonnaise, chopped parsley, salt, pepper, cayenne.

Generously stuff each tomato shell. Garnish tops with tiny parsley sprigs and a little dash of paprika.

Lobster French-American Style

1½ tbs. margarine

2 tsp. finely chopped carrots

4 tsp. finely chopped onions

1 tsp. finely chopped parsley

¼ tsp. dried thyme

½ bay leaf

1 live 1-pound lobster, cut by the market into serving
    pieces

2 tsp. salt

1 tsp. vegetable oil

2⅔ tsp. cognac

2 tsp. finely chopped shallots or scallions

¼ cup dry white wine

¼ cup chicken stock (fresh or canned)

1 medium-size tomato, peeled, seeded and coarsely
    chopped (about ½ cup)

½ tsp. tomato paste

1 tsp. bottled meat extract

1 tsp. lemon juice

½ tsp. finely cut fresh tarragon or ⅙ tsp. crumbled
dried tarragon
salt and freshly ground black pepper

In a heavy 2-quart flameproof casserole, melt ¾ tbs. margarine over moderate heat. When foam subsides, stir in carrots and onions; cook, stirring, for 5 to 8 minutes until they are soft but not brown. Remove from the heat. Stir in half the parsley, the thyme and the bay leaf.

Scoop out the greenish-brown tomalley (or liver) from the lobster and set aside. If there is black roe (or coral), save it. Sprinkle lobster with 2 tsp. salt. Then heat the oil almost to smoking point in heavy medium-size skillet and sauté lobster over high heat, turning frequently until shell is red. Remove all but a film of oil from skillet and remove from the heat. Flame the lobster with cognac that has been heated in small saucepan over a low heat, a little at a time. Shake skillet gently until flame dies. Using tongs, transfer lobster pieces to casserole. Pour juices from skillet over them, and stir in tomatoes and shallots.

In the same skillet, combine wine, stock, tomato, tomato paste and meat extract. Bring this to a boil, stirring constantly. Boil 2 minutes; then pour it over the lobster.

Stir contents of casserole together until all lobster pieces are coated with sauce. Bring to a boil over high heat. Then cover casserole tightly and simmer for 30 minutes, basting 3 or 4 times with the juices.

Meanwhile, cream the remaining ¾ tbs. margarine by beating it against sides of a bowl with a wooden spoon until it is fluffy. Beat in the tomalley, coral, lemon juice, tarragon, remaining ½ tsp. parsley and a little salt and pepper. Press through a sieve and set aside. When the lobster is done, arrange the pieces on a heated soup plate and set it in a 250° oven to keep it warm. Strain the entire contents of the casserole through a fine sieve into a 1-quart saucepan, pressing down on vegetables with a spoon, then throw out what's left in the sieve. Boil juices over high heat until reduced to about half.

Turn heat low and beat in creamed margarine mixture. Very gradually cook sauce over low heat 5 minutes; do not let it boil. Taste for seasoning. Pour sauce over lobster.

Exercise One / To Limber Up

Stand straight with your back to the wall, feet apart and six inches away from the wall. Inhale and lift your arms straight over your head, being sure to pull in your abdomen as you do. Bend forward from the waist, exhaling as you do. Inhale as you roll back up along the wall, one vertebra at a time. As your arms return to the overhead position, be sure to stretch out your neck so that your head is high. Pulling down and back on your shoulders helps. Repeat 10 times.

Exercise Two / For Waist

Stand straight. Clasp hands with arms extended from the waist. Inhaling and exhaling, rotate your upper body in wide circles from the waist, first to the right, then to the left. Repeat 10 times in each direction and work up to 20 times.

Exercise Three / For Inner Thighs

Lie flat on floor with hands under bottom, palms down. Inhale and with your legs wide apart lift them slowly in the air. Exhale as you lower them slowly. Start with 5 times and work up to 20.

Exercise Four / For Abdomen

Sit on floor, legs extended and hands clasped behind your head. Lift legs from floor about two inches and move your legs as if you were bicycling. Inhale and exhale sharply as you do this exercise. Repeat 5 times and work up to 20. Try to keep your body erect from the waist up while doing this exercise.

Exercise Five / For Back

Stand on floor. Extend arms straight in front of you and hold on to the back of a chair or a dresser. Inhale as you draw right knee up toward chest, keeping your left leg straight. Now exhale slowly as you bend forward and extend your right leg behind you. Slowly return foot to floor. Repeat this exercise 10 times with each leg and work up to 20 times each.

Exercise Six / For Circulation

Stand straight and sink into a one-third knee bend, keeping

back straight. Place hands on hips and hop on balls of feet 10
times, inhaling and exhaling as you do. Work up to 20 times.

The Portable Hair Style

Have you wondered why models look so different in each picture, while plain old you seem to look the same day in and day out? It's a very discouraging thought—but like so many others, this secret of the professional beauties is available to you too.

Models have great wardrobes of hair; they have to look different all the time. As a person who travels a great deal, I have at least a dozen hairpieces that are always set, ready to be put on. And as a person who appears in public often, I too like to change my look, and I don't always have time to set my hair or have it set. I can, however, send my hairpieces to the hairdresser and have them come back ready to use.

Now, I know not everyone can afford a lot of hairpieces. It's a lovely thought, but not always practical for the budget. So let's think about a hairpiece that could give you the greatest possible service. By that I mean the greatest variety of hair styles. When you look at the hair counter in any store, the range of offerings is bewildering; but from where I sit, the fall is the best choice for anyone who is going to have one hairpiece only. When selecting it, make sure that it matches your own hair exactly.

There are endless styles to be created with a fall. You can let it hang loosely around your face, or you can casually toss it back with your head. The ever-chic chignon and George Washington take very little time to make with a fall.

Lots of women don't buy hairpieces because they're afraid that they'll fall off, but I'm going to banish those fears right now. Here's how to do it.

> 1. Make a part across the top of your head about two inches in back of your hairline. Let the hair in front of the part hang down on your face.
> 2. Next, if your hairpiece has no comb with which to fasten it, make a couple of pin curls and fasten your hairpiece as shown on page 137.
> 3. Now brush the front hair back over the hairpiece. Spray with hair spray to hold in place. To become really expert with a hairpiece takes a little practice. The time it saves and the hairdos you can achieve make the learning worth the effort.

Study and learn the various effects you can create with your hairpiece—from gypsy to gentlewoman, depending on your whim. Be tempting, or insouciant—the mood is up to you: you, the newly awakened woman that you've become.

Day XII

Menu

Breakfast

> 1,000 units Vitamin C and 1 therapeutic multiple-vitamin capsule with minerals
> 1 or 2 slices smoked salmon

Lunch

> 1 or 2 slices broiled filet of sole

Dinner

> Clam broth (bottled).
> Grilled halibut steak
> 1 glass of white wine, if desired

* Do not forget eight glasses of liquids!

Broiled Filet of Sole

1 or 2 slices filet of sole
1 tbs. margarine
paprika
salt

Heat broiler at BROIL for 15 minutes. Place fish on foil that covers broiling pan. Dot with margarine and cover with another piece of foil. Place in broiler for 15 minutes. Remove from broiler, uncover and sprinkle with paprika. Return pan to broiler for another 5 minutes. Remove from heat and salt to taste.

Grilled Halibut Steak

halibut steak, 1 inch or ½ inch thick
anchovy margarine
salt
freshly ground black pepper
½ cucumber, chopped and cooked in 3 tbs. melted
    margarine for 5 minutes

Heat broiler at BROIL for 15 minutes. Make anchovy margarine by mixing ½ tsp. of anchovy paste with one tbs. of margarine. Spread on both sides of fish. Season the fish with a little salt and freshly ground black pepper. Place on oiled foil on the broiling pan and put it about 3 inches from the flame. Cook on each side until brown; this will take from 3 to 5 minutes depending on the thickness of the fish. When the halibut is cooked, pour the cucumber and margarine over it.

Exercise One / To Limber Up

Sit on floor and inhale as you raise your arms overhead. Keeping your legs together, exhale as you lower your body to your legs, reaching as far as you can, grasping your legs and holding for a count of 3. Release, and inhale as you return to starting position. Repeat 3 times and work up to 5.

Exercise Two / For Waist

Sit on the floor with legs extended. Pull right foot in with knee bent so that sole of right foot touches inside of left leg. Place right hand behind you, palm on the floor. Reach forward with left hand on left ankle, exhaling as you do. Now move in semicircle, keeping your back arched and allowing your head to fall back. Return by making semicircle in the direction from which you came. Repeat 10 times on each side.

153

Exercise Three / For Thighs

Lie on back on floor with arms outstretched. Inhale as you lift your legs together straight up. Now exhale as you lower your legs about a quarter of the way to the right. Hold for a count of 3. Inhale, return to the starting position and repeat on the left. Each pair of movements counts for 1. Repeat 10 times and work up to 20.

Exercise Four / For Legs

Lie on your left side, left arm extended, balancing yourself with your right hand in front of you on floor about waist level. Raise your legs about an inch or two above the floor. Swing them in a scissors kick, inhaling and exhaling as you do. Repeat exercise 10 times on each side.

Exercise Five / For Back

Lie on stomach on floor, arms extended in front of you. Lift legs behind you and do a small scissors kick. Do this 10 times and work up to 20. This is really tough to do. It helps to raise the chest a little. It's a great back strengthener.

Exercise Six / For Circulation

Stand straight, arms extended straight out to the sides, palms down. Bend body slightly forward from waist. Raise yourself to the balls of your feet. Hop on toes, and kick legs alternately, knees straight, sharply to the rear. Inhale and exhale sharply as you perform this movement. Repeat 10 times and work up to 20.

Keep Your "Hair" Looking Fabulous

Just because you possess a wig or hairpiece or even several of each, don't think that you have the Open, sesame! to beauty. Your "hair" needs the same loving treatment that you give your very own mane. That means it should be kept clean, set and ready to go in a minute. The main difference between your head and your "hair" is that your "hair" should always be in rollers when not on your head. Endless questions have been asked about how to keep hairpieces and wigs in working order, and it really isn't very complicated.

If they're handmade of great hair, they should be dry-cleaned. That doesn't mean you send them off to the dry cleaner with your clothes. Buy some dry-cleaning fluid (nonflammable and nontoxic), pour it into a bowl and dip the pieces into the bowl, following the directions on the can. Then air them thoroughly until the smell is gone.

If they're machine-made hairpieces, either of synthetic fiber or of real hair, they should just be washed. You could use ordinary shampoo, but my models seem to prefer Ivory or Lux flakes.

Once your hairpieces are clean, they should be set at once. The best way to set them is to keep them in rollers, on head stands (which you can buy in most notion departments and five-and-ten-cent stores). Cover the hairpieces on the stands with chiffon scarfs to keep them in glorious shape, for if you toss them on chairs or stuff them in boxes, they're going to look just as if you tossed them on chairs or stuffed them in boxes— not at all part of the glorious new picture!

It's really no work at all to keep your "hair" looking great every minute, and if you're going to play the beauty game, play it all the way.

Menu

Breakfast

        1,000 units Vitamin C and 1 therapeutic multiple-vitamin capsule with minerals

        ½ or whole cold lobster with lemon juice (2 tbs.)

Lunch

        Sautéed scallops

Dinner

        3 pieces marinated herring (bought in store)

        Moules Marinière

        1 glass of white wine, if desired

* Do not forget your eight glasses of liquids!

Sautéed Scallops

18 or 24 bay scallops
3 tbs. margarine
1 tsp. finely chopped garlic
1 tsp. tomato paste
salt and pepper to taste

Wash scallops in water and pat dry with paper towels.

Heat margarine, garlic and tomato paste slowly—very slowly —so that the margarine absorbs the flavor of the garlic and tomato paste. When the mixture begins to bubble, add the scallops and sauté them about eight minutes. Add salt and freshly ground pepper to taste.

Moules Marinière

1 pt. mussels (You can eat pints or quarts—it doesn't
    matter how many.)
1 cup white wine
1 finely chopped shallot
1 tbs. margarine
1 tbs. finely chopped parsley

Scrub mussels well and pull off their beards. Place mussels in saucepan; add margarine, white wine and shallot. Cover and cook over brisk flame until shells open. Remove mussels from saucepan and serve in soup bowl covered with broth, which has been brought to a boil for 10 minutes. Sprinkle mussels with parsley.

Exercise One / To Limber Up

Sit on the floor with your legs straight and spread apart. In-hale as you stretch both arms overhead. Keep your left arm straight and slide it down along your left leg. Your eventual aim is to touch your head to your knee. Keep your right arm stretched upward and behind your ear. Exhale as you slide slowly forward. Inhale as you return to arms-overhead position. Repeat to right, keeping left arm up. Repeat 10 times to each side, working up to 20.

Exercise Two / For Waist

Lie on back on floor, arms stretched out to sides. Inhale. Raise right leg, cross it over and try to touch it to left hand, exhaling as you do. Inhale as you return to starting position. Now try to touch left leg to your right hand. Each pair of exercises counts as 1. Repeat 10 times and work up to 20.

Exercise Three / For Inner Thighs

Lie on back, arms at sides. Inhale. Lift legs straight in the air and open them slowly out to the sides, exhaling as you do. Hold for a count of 3. Inhale as you return to legs-closed-and-elevated position. Repeat 10 times and work up to 20.

Exercise Four / For Abdomen

Lie on back. Raise legs until they are three-quarters of the way up. Inhaling and exhaling sharply, kick legs quickly back and forth, never allowing feet to go more than six inches apart. Be sure that your stomach muscles are contracted during this exercise. Repeat 10 times and work up to 20.

Exercise Five / For Calves and Back of Thighs

Stand straight, arms extended straight in front of you. Rise up on balls of feet, inhaling as you do. Remaining on balls of feet, exhale as you sink into deep knee bend. Arms should remain extended throughout this movement. Inhale as you return to starting position, still on balls of feet. Repeat 10 times and work up to 20. (You can balance on back of a chair if necessary.)

Exercise Six / For Circulation

Stand straight on balls of feet. Bounce twice, and on third bounce try to kick yourself in the bottom. Inhale and exhale quickly during the exercise. Repeat 10 times and work up to 20. Each set of three jumps counts as 1.

Kissable Fingers

When the moment comes for hand holding, is the hand you reach out crowned with lovely tapered fingernails, or does your hand resemble a paw? No matter what you do—even if you're a lady riveter—there is no reason to have unsightly fingernails. How can you tickle a man's neck, reach out to stroke his cheek or, for that matter, play bridge if your fingernails are not perfection?

Do you think that all models have long nails? Some do, some don't. Those that have them can crack or break them. Imagine a model showing up for a cosmetic picture with fingernails that are anything less than perfection. The client would take his $60 or $75 an hour, put it in his pocket and go away furious. Imagine a duke about to kiss a duchess's hand and seeing, as he does, some broken-off stubs where the nails were. He'd drop the proffered pinkies in a flash. Even duchesses can crack or break nails.

Well, it need not happen that way anymore. Models get their pictures taken and duchesses get their hands kissed because they share a secret. The secret is Kadon powder and liquid, which can be purchased in any dental-supply store. It's a substance used by some dentists to fill teeth, and it can patch cracked nails or, for that matter, make new ones for you. Here's a list of supplies you will need:

1. Kadon powder
2. Kadon liquid
3. Emery board
4. A small piece of silver foil folded into a semicircle to fit under the end of your nail
5. 2 bottle caps or small-size aluminum caps to use as containers
6. nail-polish remover
7. cuticle cream or liquid remover
8. nail-polish brush

To make a false nail, follow these steps:

1. Remove old nail polish, then wash and dry fingernails.
2. Put a small quantity of Kadon powder in a container.
3. Place an equal amount of Kadon liquid in another container.
4. Take the semicircle you have made from silver foil. Moisten it a little bit with water and gently place it under the end of your nail, or where your nail should be (see page 159).
5. Dip the brush into the liquid until it is saturated. Then dip it into the powder. Place powder on your nail and brush the mixture onto the silver form. Keep repeating this process until you have formed a nail. It will look very long and ugly.
6. Let nail dry for at least 5 minutes.
7. Gently remove silver form.
8. With emery board, smooth the surface of the nail and then file it into the shape you like.

9. Clean the nail with a small amount of polish remover. Make sure to go around the cuticle carefully.

10. Wash and dry hands thoroughly.

11. You're ready for a manicure!

If you've broken a nail and you think it's beyond repair, you're in for a great surprise, because you can easily patch the break with the same powder and liquid—simply by brushing the powder and liquid over the nail. The patch will normally last until the nail grows out.

If either the patch or the nail starts to loosen, soak your fingernail in polish remover for about five minutes; then you can easily peel off the loose patch or nail and, if necessary, make another.

Imagine the look of long, lovely fingers holding a cup as you linger over your coffee. The hands of the patrician lady, the hands of the professional model are now yours. Use them gracefully, slowly, thoughtfully. You'll be surprised one day to see that all these little things are going to go into the making of a completely new person—you!

Day XIV

Halibut

Margarine

garlic

Knife

chopped garlic.

Powdered Tarragon

tsp.

S p

paste of garlic, tarragon margarine

greased foil

wrap

Menu

Breakfast

1,000 units of Vitamin C and 1 therapeutic multiple-
vitamin capsule with minerals
8 cold boiled shrimp

Lunch

2 slices broiled sole

Dinner

Crab cocktail (4 oz.) with cocktail sauce (Use fresh,
frozen or canned crabmeat.)
Halibut baked in foil
1 glass of white wine, if desired

* Do not forget eight glasses of liquids!

Halibut Baked in Foil

½ lb. halibut (or any other firm, white fish)
1 tbs. margarine
⅛ tsp. garlic, chopped very fine
⅛ tsp. powdered tarragon
salt and pepper to taste

Preheat oven to 350°. Wash fish and dry with paper towels. Mix the margarine, garlic and tarragon to a consistency that will spread easily; rub on each side of fish. With a little extra margarine, grease one side of a piece of aluminum foil large enough to wrap around the fish; place fish on buttered side of foil and fold tightly so that fish is completely enclosed. Bake in oven for 35–40 minutes, and serve.

Exercise One / To Limber Up

Sit up straight on floor with your hands beside your hips, palms down, and your left leg extended straight in front of you. Now bend right knee and draw right foot up as much as possible on top of your left leg. Inhaling and exhaling sharply, push your right knee down to floor, then allow to return to starting position. Eventually you will be able to place your foot on your thigh while your knee is flat on the floor. Do this 10 times and reverse.

Exercise Two / For Waist

Stand with legs apart, hands clasped behind your neck. Lift your right knee and bring your left elbow down to touch it, exhaling as you do so. Inhale as you return to starting position. Repeat touching left knee to right elbow. Repeat 10 times to each side, working up to 20 each side.

Exercise Three / For Upper Abdomen

Lie on back, arms extended behind your head on the floor. Inhale. Curl your head and neck forward as you swing your arms forward and pull your knees up and in toward your chest, exhaling as you do. Repeat 5 times and work up to 20.

Exercise Four / For Lower Abdomen

Lie on back on floor, legs apart, arms stretched out to sides. Inhale. Keeping arms outstretched, pull the body forward from the waist up and lift your legs in the air as you do. Exhale as you move quickly forward. Inhale as you roll slowly back. Repeat 3 times and work up to 20.

Exercise Five / For Back and Waist

Stand straight, hands at sides, legs together. In a swift, forceful motion raise your stiffened right arm and stiffened left leg up and backward; hold for a second, then return. The motion should be very strong. Then raise stiffened left arm and right leg up and backward. Repeat each pair of movements—first one side, then the other—10 times. Work up to 20.

Exercise Six / For Circulation

Stand straight, feet together, hands on hips. Inhaling and exhaling, rapidly jump on balls of feet first to the right, then to the center, then to the left, then to the center, then to the right. Each four positions count as 1 hop. Repeat 10 times.

Touchable Toes

While you're being admired, you might just as well be admired all over. By that I mean from top to toe. How does that get you? Can you face the toe test? Are your feet pedicured and pampered as they should be?

Many years ago, when I was in my early twenties, I was invited to a party at *Vogue* magazine. It was just before Christmas, and I'd been working very hard. The party started at noon, so I rushed over from my office inky-fingered, stringy-haired and in general, looking as if I had been shot out of a cannon. I was introduced to the publisher. Mr. Iva Patcevitch, who took my grubby hand with the chipped nail polish in his hand, looked in my eyes and said, "You should always be feminine, my dear. Even your toes should be perfectly polished." If I could have crawled into a hole I would have, for inside my scuffed suede pumps were feet that had the traces of last summer's nail polish on the toenails! Did he have X-ray eyes? Not at all. As I've learned since, a mess is just a mess. It was a moment that changed my life. From that day to this I've never been without a perfect manicure or pedicure, and neither should you be.

Being feminine is not a responsibility that you can shrug off with excuses: either you are or you're not. When you are feminine, people delight in you; when you're not, they're usually too polite to tell you the truth. So take those feet that you've got hidden out of sight by now and start caring for them today. A pedicure need be given only as often as you need one. You'll find the average duration about three weeks.

Here's a list of what you'll need:

1. Nail brush
2. Pumice stone
3. Body moisture
4. Toenail clippers
5. Emery board
6. Cuticle cream or oil
7. Orange stick
8. Polish remover
9. Nail polish
10. Cotton
11. Sealer polish

Remove your toenail polish.

To begin a pedicure, you can either soak your feet as you're soaking yourself in a bath, or soak them in lovely hot water all by themselves. Scrub your feet with a nail brush; then go over them with a pumice stone that has been soaked for ten minutes in water and rubbed with soap. Rub the pumice stone all over the hard skin. (It won't hurt if you use a pumice stone on your feet daily. It really helps to keep calluses away.)

Dry your feet thoroughly, and massage them with the same body moisturizer that you use all over. Then cut your nails straight across, smooth the edges with an emery board and apply cuticle cream or oil. Push the cuticle back gently with an orangewood stick and run the stick under the nail to remove any remaining dead skin.

Now you're ready for polish. Separate your toes with wads of cotton and apply two coats, letting the first coat dry thoroughly before the second. Last, apply a sealer coat and allow that to dry thoroughly.

If your feet are really beyond your own treatment, then get yourself to a podiatrist in a hurry and let him start the rehabilitation program. The pedicure is something you can and really must take care of yourself.

You may never have thought of your feet as a part of your new feminine beauty, but they can be. No one may ever say a word until the summer when they show in sandals. Sooner or later someone will pay you the compliment you deserve, and then it will be worth all the effort.

Beginning
Third Week

. . . You're Almost There

WEIGHT	BUST	WAIST	HIPS	THIGHS

Day XV

Menu

Breakfast

1,000 units of Vitamin C and 1 therapeutic multiple-vitamin capsule with minerals

½ or whole cold lobster

Lunch

Steamed clams—12 or as many as you like (you can buy these in a can) with melted margarine

Dinner

Barcelona Seafood Stew

1 glass of white wine, if desired

* Do not forget your eight glasses of liquids!

Barcelona Seafood Stew

1-lb. live lobster—prepared by fish market as for
  bouillabaisse
1 tbs. salad oil
1 cup finely chopped onion
¾ tbs. finely chopped garlic
½ small red or green pepper, deribbed, seeded and
  finely chopped
½ tbs. finely chopped lean smoked ham
1 medium-size tomato, peeled, seeded and finely
  chopped
½ bay leaf, crumbled
pinch ground saffron threads crushed with back of
  spoon
¼ tsp. salt
freshly ground black pepper
4 cups water
1 cup dry white wine
1 tbs. fresh lemon juice
4 mussels, scrubbed and bearded (optional)
4 small clams, scrubbed

3 large raw shrimp in shell
3 sea scallops, cut in half

In a casserole, heat the salad oil over moderate heat for 5 minutes.

Add the onions, garlic and red or green pepper and cook, stirring frequently, for 5 minutes, or until the vegetables are soft. Stir in the ham and cook for a minute or two. Then add the tomato, bay leaf, saffron, salt and a little pepper. Bring to a boil and cook for about 5 minutes. Add the water, wine and lemon juice, bring to a boil and stir. Then drop in the lobster, mussels and clams. Cover the casserole tightly, reduce the heat to moderate and cook for 10 minutes. Add the shrimp and scallops; cover and cook 5 minutes longer. Discard any clams or mussels that have not opened.

Exercise One / To Limber Up

Sit on floor with legs apart in a V. Place both arms on right leg. Inhale. Slowly slide your hands down your right leg as far as possible, exhaling as you do. Return to original position, inhaling as you do. Now slide hands down left leg. Repeat 10 times with each leg; work up to 20. Your eventual goal is to touch your head to your knees.

Exercise Two / For Back of Thighs and Waist

Lie on back, arms outstretched on floor behind head. Inhale. Swing your arms up and forward and bend your body forward as if to touch your toes. Exhale as you come forward and bend from the waist, arms extended straight in front of you. Return to original position. Repeat 10 times and work up to 20.

183

Exercise Three / For Abdomen

Lie on back, arms at sides, legs together. Raise legs at a right angle to floor, inhaling deeply as you do. Then lower them slowly to the floor, stopping on the way down for a count of 3 at the one-third mark, again at the two-thirds mark. Exhale slowly in a controlled breath as you lower legs. Repeat 3 times and work up to 20. Keep at this exercise. It's worth the effort.

Exercise Four / For Inner Thighs

Lie on back, arms at sides. Raise legs up as close to perpendicular to your body as you can. Spread them; then, inhaling and exhaling sharply, cross them in the air: left under, right under, left under, right under—5 times. Work up to 20.

Exercise Five / For Calves

Stand erect, feet together. Try to lift right leg until your foot can rest on the arm of a chair or on a dresser with the leg fully extended. Inhale. Lean forward on your left leg, bending right knee, exhaling as you do. Return to starting position, inhaling as you do. Repeat 10 times and switch to other leg. Work up to 20 times.

Exercise Six | For Circulation

Hop on the balls of feet, inhaling, then exhaling, sharply with each hop, alternating feet every two hops. This is like an Indian war dance. Do this 20 times.

Golden Girl

To sun worshipers, the effective lecture on the evils of sunbathing has not been given. It's perfectly true that the sun dries your skin, can give you skin cancer and make wrinkles around your eyes. Yet few of us can resist the delicious sensation of basking in the hot sun. What a divine feeling to step off a plane in winter clothes and find oneself on a sunbathed island! Slush and cold behind you, it's a race to the sun for the first bake. Unfortunately, too many people are so anxious to get a tan that they flop right down, never mind the result.

I've heard so many people say, "I can't ever get a tan" or "I always burn first, then tan" that it's like a sun song to me. Anyone can get a tan, and no one need get a burn first; it's a question of timing. I love to get a tan, and I have olive skin that used to burn first, but not now. I've seen the fairest skin in all of Scandinavia turn golden brown under my supervision.

Tanning is a science (my kind of science, that is). You can't rush it. You've got to develop it. Once you've developed a tan, it's easier and easier to maintain it. The secret is the base. It's best to take two weeks in the winter developing a base that you can reactivate in the summer, thus preventing your skin from burning, then drying and peeling, for the sake of hearing some-

186

one admire your tan. My kind of tanning is deep and lasting, and it works like this.

You will need:

1. Plastic eye protectors
2. Nose sun block
3. Lip sun block
4. A timer with a bell
5. Suntan lotion or oil
6. A bucket of cool water
7. Body moisture
8. Face moisture
9. If you color your hair, a scarf or anything to protect it from the sun

To acquire the tan:

1. Before you go into the sun, apply suntan lotion. If you have fair, delicate skin, use a lotion that has a sunscreen agent in it. If you have dark skin, use oil; even just coconut oil will do.
2. Apply the nose-protector cream, stick or gel to your nose.
3. Apply the lip protector. (It's usually in stick form.)
4. Find a nice sunny place and lie down with your timer set for 5 minutes to 20 minutes, depending on the texture of your skin.
5. When the timer goes off, splash your face with cool water, and apply more suntan lotion. If you have lily-white or very sensitive skin, go take a cool shower to reduce your skin temperature at once. You may go back after 20 minutes in the shade.

Continue like this until your skin starts to take on a tan. The first days are crucial. Never allow your skin to burn. It's better to sit in the shade for a few hours than to ruin the entire thing with a too-quick start.

If somehow you have gotten sunburned, make a pitcher of very strong tea. Allow it to cool. Dip a face cloth or saturate a towel in the tea and place it on the sunburn. Keep the cloth wet with the tea. You can put the cooled tea bags on your closed eyelids if they have become sunburned.

A tan is really becoming. If you follow these rules *exactly*, you or anyone else can develop a tan. However, you've got to control yourself and develop it. It may seem to take an eternity, but it doesn't. Timing is *the* great secret in life, and it's the most important secret of a beautiful golden-tanned body.

Menu

Breakfast

    1,000 units of Vitamin C and 1 therapeutic multiple-vitamin capsule with minerals

    1 or 2 slices of smoked whitefish with lemon juice

Lunch

    Shrimp salad—12 shrimp mixed with 1 tsp. chopped onion, ½ cup chopped celery and 2 tbs. mayonnaise

Dinner

    Fish soup

    Per Mortensen's Grilled Mackerel

    1 glass of white wine, if desired

* Don't forget eight glasses of liquids!

Fish Soup

Fish Stock

> 2 tsp. coarsely chopped parsnips
> 4 tsp. coarsely chopped carrots
> 2 tbs. coarsely chopped yellow onion
> pinch of salt
> 1 black peppercorn
> ½ tsp. chopped parsley stems
> ⅙ bay leaf
> ½ stalk celery, with leaves or celeriac tops
> ⅓ lb. fish trimmings (heads, bones—washed)
> 2 cups cold water

Combine ingredients in medium-size saucepan; bring to boil and partially cover pan; turn heat low and simmer 30 minutes. Strain stock through fine sieve into medium-size bowl; press to get out all juices. Wash pan and return strained stock to it. Boil rapidly, uncovered, about 20 minutes.

> 2 tsp. finely chopped parsnips
> 4 tsp. finely chopped carrots

¾ lb. boneless halibut, cod or haddock, in one piece
4 tsp. finely sliced onion
1 egg yolk
pinch salt
pinch freshly ground pepper
1 tsp. finely chopped parsley

Add carrots, parsnips and fish. Bring to boil; reduce heat and simmer 10 minutes; add onion and simmer 2 or 3 minutes longer. Remove from heat; lift out fish with slotted spoon and place on heated soup plate. In small bowl, beat egg yolk with wire whisk; then beat in ½ cup of hot soup, 1 tbs. at a time. Pour this back into soup *slowly*, beating constantly with wire whisk. Break the fish with a fork and add it to soup. Keep soup hot, but do not allow to boil. Season with salt and pepper. Pour into a bowl and sprinkle with parsley.

Per Mortensen's Grilled Mackerel

1 tbs. salad oil
½ tbs. lemon juice
¼ tsp. salt
freshly ground black pepper
1 tsp. finely chopped onion
1 one-pound mackerel, filleted
1½ tbs. vegetable oil
1 tbs. margarine
1 tsp. horseradish

Preheat the broiler. In a shallow baking dish large enough to hold the fish flat, put the oil, lemon juice, salt, a little freshly ground black pepper and chopped onion. Place the fish in this marinade, flesh side down, and let stand 15 minutes; then turn it over for another 15 minutes. Brush broiler grill with ¾ tbs. of oil and place fish on it, skin side down. Grill on only one side, about 3 inches from heat, basting fish from time to time with remaining oil. In 10–12 minutes, fish should have turned a light golden color and flesh should flake easily when prodded with fork. Serve the fish with horseradish.

Exercise One | To Limber Up

Sit on floor in cross-legged position, back straight. Place hands on knees. Slowly lower chin until it touches chest. Rotate head to left, rolling it gently until you have formed a complete circle. Reverse, rolling head slowly to the right. Inhale as you begin the roll and slowly exhale as you end it, counting each two neck rolls as 1. Do the exercise 10 times.

Exercise Two | For Waist

Sit on floor, legs apart. Raise arms overhead and inhale. Exhale as you lean forward and try to touch your right hand to your left toe. Inhale as you raise body and exhale as you lean forward and reach with left hand to right toe. Repeat the pair of movements 10 times and work up to 20. Do not reach farther than is comfortable at any time.

Exercise Three / For Lower Abdomen and Inner Thighs

Lie on your back on floor, hands clasped under your head. Spread your legs wide apart. Inhale. Lift legs slowly from the floor as high as is comfortable; exhale as you lower them. Repeat 10 times and work up to 20.

Exercise Four / For Back

Lie on stomach on sturdy stool, arms stretched in front of you, legs stretched in back of you. Keep chin high to help maintain balance. Lift left arm and right leg, then right arm and left leg. Inhale and exhale sharply as you do this exercise. Repeat 10 times; work up to 20. If you are very overweight, omit this one until it is practical, and always keep near something that will prevent you from falling.

Exercise Five / For Upper Abdomen

Lie on your back on floor, hands clasped behind your head. Inhale. Roll head and shoulders forward as you quickly lift your upper body and draw up your knees. Exhale as you come forward. Straighten, then lower legs. Inhale as you roll back slowly. Repeat 3 times and work up to 20.

Exercise Six / For Circulation

Stand straight, arms extended to the sides, palms down. Bend body slightly backward from the waist. Raise yourself to balls of feet. Hop on toes, kicking one leg at a time quickly forward. Inhale and exhale sharply as you perform this exercise. Repeat 10 times and work up to 20.

Hair-free

If you've never had a good enough figure to wear a bikini before, then there's a little disadvantage to wearing one that might
not have occurred to you. That is that in a brief swimsuit one
is all too liable to expose a certain amount of pubic hair, and
it really isn't pretty. It took a lot of courage for me to write this
thought, but I feel it's so essential to your new image that I had
to tell you about it.

When the thought occurred to me, I did a little research and
found out that many women have been having bathing-suit
lines waxed at the fancier beauty salons for years. It's done the
same way leg waxing is done. Hot wax is applied to the unwanted hair and pulled off as with adhesive tape. It sounded
very painful to me, so I didn't try.

I asked some other friends who tried shaving, but apparently
this causes itching as the hair grows again. The vision of the ir-
resistible scratching that inevitably would follow was ludicrous.

The other day I came across a depilatory in a foam can. I
tried it and it worked like a charm. Believe me, you have to be
able to be very alone for one-half hour when you do this. The
results are what you want, so find the time.

    1. Either standing or lying down on the bathroom

floor, apply the depilatory to the unwanted hair. It isn't easy to determine exactly where to put the depilatory; you must look at yourself in your bathing suit from all angles to determine this.

2. Allow it to stay about 20 minutes. (The directions on the can say 7 minutes, but that wasn't long enough for me.) I have since found a more effective spray depilatory that works in 5 minutes.

3. Then remove the depilatory with damp facial tissues or a tongue depressor. Magically, the hair is gone.

4. Wash the area on which you had the depilatory thoroughly.

5. Apply body moisture.

The hair seems to reappear about two or three weeks later, so you've got to remove it again. But it's so very nice to be in shape to wear a bikini that the joys offset the tedium of removing the hair.

Menu

Breakfast

      1,000 units Vitamin C and 1 therapeutic multiple-vitamin capsule with minerals

      Cold crabmeat (4 oz.)

Lunch

      Minced-clam omelet

Dinner

      2 slices canned Matjes herring with 1 tsp. chopped onion

      Gravlax Count Claus Lewenhaupt

      1 glass of white wine, if desired

* Do not forget eight glasses of liquids!

Minced-Clam Omelet

2 eggs
1 tbs. minced onions
1 tbs. finely chopped green pepper
1 tsp. salt
2 tbs. drained canned minced clams

Beat the eggs with a wire whisk in a bowl until frothy. Add remaining ingredients; stir until well blended. Pour mixture into skillet or omelet pan and cook until golden brown. Gently flip and cook on other side until golden brown.

Gravlax Count Claus Lewenhaupt

2 pieces filleted fresh salmon, cleaned and scaled
¼ bunch fresh dill, coarsely chopped
1 tbs. coarse (kosher) salt
1 tsp. sugar
½ tsp. crushed black peppercorns
¼ lemon

Place half fish, skin side down, in a deep glass, enamel or stainless-steel baking dish. Spread the dill on the fish.

In a separate bowl combine salt, sugar and crushed peppercorns. Sprinkle mixture evenly over dill. Top with other half of fish, skin side up. Cover with aluminum foil and on top of it set something very heavy; try cans of food. Refrigerate 48 to 72 hours (just depending on when you wish to make it), basting with liquid marinade that accumulates. Be sure that you baste the halves of salmon inside as well as outside. Replace foil and weight each time.

When gravlax is finished, remove fish from sauce, scrape away dill and seasonings, remove the skin and pat dry.

Serve as is with lemon wedge (¼ lemon) or broil quickly. Either way it's fabulous.

Exercise One / To Limber Up

Stand with right foot about twelve inches in front of left foot, toes pointed outward. Clasp hands behind back. Inhale deeply. Slowly lower head toward knees, raising arms behind you straight above your head. Exhale as you bend forward and inhale as you slowly return to starting position. Repeat 10 times. Switch to left leg and repeat exercise. Work up to 20 times.

Exercise Two / For Waist

Stand up straight, feet together, arms extended over head with hands clasped. Inhale deeply. Exhale as you lift your left leg to the side and bend your body to the right. Do not try to lift leg or bend body too far; time will take care of this. Repeat 10 times and alternate legs.

Exercise Three / For Inner Thighs

Lie on back with arms stretched over head. Lift your legs straight up until they are at a right angle to your body. Spread your legs apart and move them in outward circles. Bring them back together and lower them slowly to the floor. Inhale as you raise legs, exhale as you lower them. Repeat 10 times.

Exercise Four / For Abdomen

Sit on the floor. Recline on elbows, which should be close to your body. While inhaling and exhaling quickly, raise your legs six inches from floor and kick them quickly back and forth. Do this 10 times and work up to 20.

Exercise Five / For Back

Stand straight, feet together. Bend left knee and extend right arm above your head, palm facing forward. Extend your left leg behind you and exhale as you slowly bend forward from waist, keeping back arched and head back. Try to bring your upper body parallel to the floor. Keep your arm extended during this whole movement. Return body to original position, inhaling as you do. Repeat 5 times on each leg; work up to 10.

Exercise Six / For Circulation

Squat. Place weight on balls of feet. Extend arms straight out to sides. Now hop on balls of feet, inhaling and exhaling sharply. Bounce around the room on the balls of your feet 10 times; work up to 20.

The Liberated Body

As time goes by, skin seems to dry out. The sun and time take their toll! Some people just have dry, itchy skin; others have scaly skin. I don't really know any lasting cure for the latter, but for dry, itchy, flaky skin there's lots of help to be had by bathing. The right kind of bathing can leave your new shape covered in skin that is like velvet to the touch. This kind of bathing can be done daily and is frankly luxurious in its feeling. You emerge feeling a little as Cleopatra must have felt after her bath.

You will need:

1. Pumice stone
2. Castile soap
3. Cornstarch
4. A bottle in which you have mixed half glycerine and half rosewater
5. Coconut oil
6. A back brush
7. Baby oil

You use them this way:

1. Run a warm tub into which you have put the pumice stone and one cup of cornstarch.

2. While the tub is running, massage your body with baby oil.

3. Soak in the tub for 15 minutes before washing with castile soap.

4. Scrub your back with a back brush.

5. Put soap on the pumice stone and go lightly over your entire body. Then rinse and get out of tub.

6. When you have dried yourself, apply the glycerine-rosewater mixture to your entire body.

7. If there are any especially dry parts to your body, wait a few minutes and massage coconut oil into your skin.

This treatment will leave your skin feeling so soft and luscious that you'll find it hard to believe. Even if you have normal body skin, the change in texture after bathing this way for a week is astonishing. After a month your skin takes on a patina and slightly shiny glow. Your body feels free, liberated—which indeed it is.

Day XVIII

Menu

Breakfast

1,000 units Vitamin C and 1 therapeutic multiple-vitamin capsule with minerals

1 or 2 slices of smoked salmon

Lunch

Baked Clams Oreganata

Dinner

Shrimp cocktail

Red Snapper Trinidad

1 glass of white wine, if desired

* Don't forget eight glasses of liquids!

Baked Clams Oreganata

1 dozen clams (medium size)
2 tbs. chopped onion
2 tsp. chopped parsley
2 tsp. oregano
4 tbs. salad oil
salt and pepper to taste

Preheat oven to 375°. Open the clams; sprinkle them with onion, salt and pepper. Mix together the parsley, oregano and salad oil; pour over the clams and bake until the clams curl a bit at the edges. You can eat 12 or 24 of these; they're not at all fattening.

Red Snapper Trinidad

1 tsp. salad oil
1 tbs. coarsely chopped onion
2 pimento-stuffed olives, cut in small pieces
1 tbs. coarsely chopped canned pimento
¾ tsp. ground coriander seeds
1 tbs. fresh orange juice
½ tbs. fresh lime juice
pinch of salt
freshly ground black pepper
2 tsp. soft margarine
½-lb. red snapper, cleaned (or any firm white fish)
1 finely chopped hard-boiled egg

Preheat the oven to 400°.

In a heavy 8-inch skillet, heat the salad oil. Add the onion and cook over moderate heat, stirring frequently, for 5 minutes or until the onions are soft and clear, but not brown.

Stir in the olives, pimento and coriander seeds. Cook, stirring occasionally, for 4 minutes longer. Now add orange juice, lime juice, salt and a few grindings of black pepper.

With half the soft margarine grease the bottom and sides of

a shallow, heatproof casserole large enough to hold the fish. Put the fish in the casserole, cover with remaining margarine and pour the sauce over it. Bake uncovered, in the middle of the oven, for 30 minutes, basting the fish with the sauce every 10 minutes. The fish is done if the flesh feels firm when pressed with a finger. Do not overcook.

I serve the baked fish directly from the casserole, sprinkled with chopped egg.

Exercise One / To Limber Up

Sit on heels on floor. Place hands, palms down, at either side of toes. Slowly raise your bottom from heels, arching back and allowing your head to sink back between shoulder blades. Inhale as you raise body. Slowly sink down on heels and straighten body to starting position, exhaling as you do. Repeat 10 times. I do not think you have to do this more than 10 times ever.

Exercise Two / For Waist

Sit on floor, body erect and legs extended straight in front of you. Clasp hands behind head. Inhale, now exhale as you bend forward as far as possible. Someday you will be able to touch your forehead to your knees. Repeat 10 times and work up to 20.

Exercise Three / For Upper Abdomen

Lie on floor, arms stretched back behind head. Inhale. Swing forward and upward, exhaling as you reach forward toward your toes. Inhale as you slowly return to starting position. Repeat 10 times.

Exercise Four / For Thighs and Back of Legs

Squat with your hands between your legs and your palms on the floor. Inhaling as you do, straighten your legs as far as you can, keeping your hands flat on the floor. Exhale as you return to squatting position. Repeat 10 times, working up to 20. It does not matter if you cannot stand up with your legs straight; you will find that you can in time.

Exercise Five / For Whole Abdomen

Lie on floor with hands on thighs, palms down. Inhale deeply. Slowly curl your body forward to a one-quarter sitting position, exhaling and sliding hands along legs as you do. Be sure heels remain on floor. Slowly uncurl body and return to lying-down position, inhaling as you do. Repeat 5 times and work up to 20. This is my favorite abdominal exercise.

Exercise Six / For Circulation

Stand straight, feet together. Jump up on the balls of your feet, and when you lightly land on them, do as deep a knee bend as you can. Be careful to keep your balance and move lightly. Inhale and exhale as you hop up, hop down. Repeat this exercise 10 times and work up to 20.

Sleeping Beauty

In Latin countries business stops in the middle of the day and everyone goes home to take a nap or just rest. Having recharged their bodies' batteries, they go back to work completely renewed. No wonder the people of all these countries are known for their sunny dispositions. They've learned long ago that rest is essential to their well-being. If you have a chance, look at their faces, clear eyes, unlined skin, relaxed bodies. They know how to live.

I'm not suggesting that we change our entire business structure and take up the noontime siesta. I am, however, reminding us all that sleep is the fountain of youth.

When you're asleep, your whole system is resting, even your skin. Your metabolic rate slows down, and you are storing up, not using up, energy. Everything is being revitalized. You can apply all the creams in the world, but nothing will repair the ravages caused by lack of sleep.

Consider the siesta, if practical. It's one of the greatest youth retainers there is. But to most of us the idea of lying down for an hour or two in midday or afternoon is impractical. Yet there are few of us who can't find fifteen minutes at the end of the day, before dinner, for a rest. Some people can fall asleep for fifteen minutes and wake up feeling completely renewed. Some people can't sleep—or if they do, it ruins their dispositions or their night's sleep. For them, fifteen minutes lying down with closed eyes can be the revitalizer they need. Lying down combined with some slow, deep, even breathing is a fantastic restorer.

The amount of time one sleeps is dependent on the individual. You don't have to be asleep for eight hours to refresh yourself. I've heard that the hours you sleep before midnight are the most important. I have a suspicion that this is true only if you're a nine-to-five-thirty worker. I find that six hours is about the length of time I sleep; after that I just stay in bed with my eyes closed, breathing deeply. Often I will fall back asleep. However, every Sunday night I take a sleeping pill and go to sleep at nine o'clock in the evening. This gives me exactly what I need for the week.

I've read that some of the world's greatest beauties stay in a darkened room one day a week; they feel that this time revitalizes their entire being. Even if I could do that, it would drive me mad. But the principle is understandable: they are giving their systems a rest—the rest that helps keep the skin elastic and the eyes bright. It also keeps them away from people who are a drain on their energy. To take a lesson from these beauties isn't difficult. Whenever possible—maybe just a Saturday or Sunday morning—stay quietly alone in your room doing nothing. Call it vegetating if you will; I call it recharging. If it helps keep these women looking young when most women look old, why not let some sleep and quiet do the same for you?

Two of New York's top plastic surgeons live near us in the country. Both are married to former Ford models, and both of them agree that sleep and rest are an essential component of beauty preservation.

Take a look at your own life-style. Do you take the time to recharge yourself during the day? Do you get enough sleep to keep your skin young and pliable? Are your eyes reddened from reading or watching television until late at night? If you're not resting and sleeping as you should, then you are running yourself down faster than need be, and none of us needs that. We need all the help we can get.

Drink deep from the fountain of youth that is sleep. You'll face the world with a younger face for a lot longer time.

Day XIX

Menu

Breakfast

1,000 units Vitamin C and 1 therapeutic multiple-vitamin capsule with minerals

Smoked trout (either the half you froze or a whole trout)

Lunch

1 large cold canned artichoke bottom with shrimp salad (You really can have 2 or 3 if you're starving.)

Dinner

Ceviche Yacht *Caribe*

Calamari in tomato sauce

1 glass of white wine, if desired

* Do not forget your eight glasses of liquids!

Ceviche Yacht Caribe

¼ cup fresh or reconstituted lime juice

¼ cup fresh or reconstituted lemon juice

1 dried chili, seeded and powdered with mortar and
  pestle

½ red onion, very finely chopped

⅛ tsp. finely chopped garlic

¼ tsp. salt

freshly ground black pepper

½ lb. filet of sole cut into 1-inch squares

6 leaves of lettuce washed, dried and chilled

½ fresh hot red chili, washed, split, seeded, deribbed
  and cut lengthwise into thin strips (or use one from
  a jar)

In a medium-size bowl, mix the lime and lemon juice, powdered dried chili, chopped onion, garlic, salt and a few grindings
of pepper.

Place the fish in a flat glass or ceramic dish (do not use a
metal dish; it may affect the flavor of the fish), and pour the
marinade over it. If the marinade does not cover the fish, add
more fruit juice. Cover and refrigerate for 3 hours, or until the

fish is white and opaque, indicating that it is fully "cooked." Shape the lettuce leaves into a bowl or cup, or on a plate. Place the marinated fish in the center and garnish with onion rings and strips of fresh chili. Serve cold.

Calamari in Tomato Sauce

6 oz. very small squid
2 tbs. salad oil
¼ clove garlic
¼ cup tomato sauce (any prepared kind)
pinch of basil
2 tbs. dry white wine
¼ tsp. salt
pinch dried ground red pepper

Ask your fish dealer to skin the squid and clean it for you, or you can buy it frozen. Wash thoroughly. Heat the oil in a deep skillet; brown the garlic in it; discard the garlic. Add the squid; cook over medium heat for 10 minutes. Add the tomato sauce, basil, wine, salt and red pepper. Cover and cook over low heat for 15 minutes.

If the whole idea of squid jars you, you may substitute any other fish recipe here.

Exercise One | To Limber Up

Sit on floor, hands clasped behind head. Inhale. Keeping body erect, slowly lower body, with head going toward knees, exhaling as you do. Do not go any farther than is comfortable. Slowly return to upright position. Repeat 10 times.

Exercise Two | For Waist

Stand with feet apart and raise hands high above head, inhaling. When you have breathed as deeply as you can, twist body to the right and bend, exhaling, to touch your right toes with fingers of both hands. Raise body, inhaling, to standing position. Repeat exercise to the left. Start with 5 times on each side to make 10. Work up to 20 times (10 on each side).

Exercise Three | For Abdomen

Lie on back with hands clasped behind your head. Inhale.

Curl your upper body forward, exhaling as you do, with the eventual goal of having your forehead touch your knees. However, at first go no farther forward than is comfortable. Inhale as you return to original position. Repeat 10 times and work up to 20.

Exercise Four / For Back

Stand straight, hands at sides, legs together. Forcefully and quickly raise right arm and right leg in back of you. Hold a second. Both arm and leg must be stiff and straight. Return to first position. Repeat on left side. Inhale and exhale deeply as you do this exercise. Repeat each pair of arm and leg lifts 10 times, working up to 20.

Exercise Five / For Calves

Squat with weight resting on balls of feet. Place hands flat on floor, with arms between legs. Chin should be touching chest. Slowly straighten legs, keeping palms flat and pressing heels to floor. Inhale as you do this, and exhale as you return to squatting position. Do not expect to be able to straighten legs completely for quite a while. Repeat 5 times and work up to 20.

Exercise Six / For Circulation

Stand erect. Extend arms in front of you, palms down. Squat and then jump up to balls of feet and bounce twice. Return to squatting position. Repeat 10 times, inhaling and exhaling as you do. Work up to 20 times.

The Uncomplaining Woman

There is nothing worse than asking someone how she feels and having her tell you. "My sinus," "my hay fever," "my aching back" are really frightful bores. Don't complain. Even if you are plagued by minor or major afflictions, no one wants to hear about it.

Still, it's hard to look pretty when you do suffer from backache, and it's hard to keep from talking about it. The best thing to do is get rid of it as painlessly as possible.

Sometimes I used to find myself with a backache at the end of the day. I don't have any idea where that backache came from, but I had it for years. I would generally look and feel miserable. One day I was in the country and that back of mine was being particularly ornery, so I lay flat on the library floor, hoping it would pass.

A friend of my husband's came over to pick him up for tennis. Needless to say, he asked why I was lying on the floor. I explained about my back. He answered that he had had a back like mine for years and had spent untold sums of money on doctors, one of whom had finally given him a simple trick to do daily. It had cured his back, and it cured mine.

Lie on the floor with your buttocks touching the baseboard,

your legs straight up at right angles to your body, so that the back of your legs and heels rests against the wall.

Stay in this position for five minutes a day (see page 217).

I know it sounds foolish, but doing that simple trick daily for a few weeks will cure most backaches. It did mine and has worked for lots of friends. It can work for you and yours, too. Even more than eliminating your backache, it will forever banish that awful bit of conversation from your repertoire.

Menu

Breakfast

    1,000 units Vitamin C and 1 therapeutic multiple-vita-
      min capsule with minerals
    1 or 2 slices smoked salmon

Lunch

    12 or 18 grilled oysters

Dinner

    1 cup bottled clam broth
    Shrimp curry (no rice)
    1 glass of white wine, if desired

* Don't forget eight glasses of liquids!

Shrimp Curry

12 boiled shrimp
1 tsp. finely chopped onion
½ tsp. margarine
¼ tsp. good curry powder
pinch powdered ginger
⅙ chili, sliced
salt to taste
4 tsp. meat stock or broth
⅙ medium cucumber, diced
½ tsp. lemon juice
pinch cayenne
3 tbs. water in which shrimp were cooked

Cook the onion in the margarine until it barely starts to turn brown. Stir in the curry powder (you can add more or less to taste), the ginger, the chili and the salt (to taste). Pour the meat stock over the mixture and simmer it gently for 15 minutes, stirring it from time to time. Add the shrimp, the cucumber, the lemon juice, the cayenne, the shrimp stock. Simmer until the vegetables are tender. Serve with hot lime chutney (you can get it in most grocery shops).

Grilled Oysters

12 or 18 freshly opened oysters (Have the fish market
    do this for you.)
2 slices bacon
¼ cup minced shallots
¼ cup parsley
1 teaspoon lemon juice
1 dash Worcestershire sauce
2 drops Tabasco sauce

Preheat oven to 400°.

Place drained oysters on deep half of each shell. Arrange
filled oystershells on a layer of rock salt in a large baking dish.
Fry bacon until crisp, drain and crumble. To 3 tbs. of bacon fat
add shallots and celery and cook until almost tender. Add parsley, lemon juice, Worcestershire and Tabasco. Spoon mixture
onto oysters in the shells and top with the crumbled bacon. Bake
10 minutes.

Exercise One / To Limber Up

Lie on stomach on the floor. Place your palms on floor, fingers pointing in, under your upper chest. Inhaling deeply, slowly raise your chest and shoulders as high as you can, pressing down on your hands. Arch your spine as you raise your chest and shoulders, and allow your head to sink back. Do not raise hips from the floor. When arms are fully extended, hold this position for a count of 3; then slowly return to original position, exhaling as you do. Repeat 10 times.

Exercise Two / For Waist

Sit on the floor with legs apart and stretched in front of you. Clasp your arms behind your head and inhale. Twist your body to the right and try to touch your left elbow to your right knee, exhaling as you do. Return to starting position, inhaling as you do. Now twist to the left and try to touch your right elbow to your left knee. Do this exercise 10 times on each side and work up to 20 on each side.

Exercise Three | For Abdomen

Lie on back on floor, arms extended behind head. Inhale deeply. Roll your body up from the waist and at the same time lift your legs straight up from the floor, exhaling as you do. Your eventual aim is to touch your fingers to your toes. Start with 3 times and work up to 20. (Progress is and should be really slow, but you'll feel great when you finally master this exercise. I'm sure I will too!)

Exercise Four | For Legs

Kneel on floor with hands clasped, palms up, on floor in front of you. Place head in palms of hands. Now, inhaling slowly, push up with feet, straightening legs. This should resemble a semi-headstand. Exhale as you slowly return to starting position. Repeat 10 times.

Exercise Five | For Back

Lie on stomach on floor, hands under your thighs. Raise your head and shoulders from the floor. Do a small flutter kick. Repeat 10 times and work up to 20.

Exercise Six | For Circulation

Stand straight, legs astride, hands on hips. Inhale and bend forward from waist so that back is parallel to the floor. Bounce upper body twice, exhaling as you do. Straighten up, inhaling. Then, keeping hands on hips, lean to the left as far as you can and bounce twice, exhaling as you do. Return to upright position, inhaling. Lean backward; bounce twice, exhaling as you do. Straighten up, inhaling. Then lean to the right and bounce. Repeat entire cycle 10 times and work up to 20. Move quickly during the exercise.

Do You Smell As Good As You Look?

Tomorrow is the last day of your crash beauty program, and I want to ask a question. Do you always smell as good as you look? What part does perfume play in your life? I know that by now you're looking great. But in being completely feminine, have you considered perfume as a necessary part of the new you? It is. Perfume, that final touch to the all-woman, can be one of the sexiest things about her (ask any man!)—or even one of the prettiest, most shocking, most mysterious—according to her mood, and according to the perfume she chooses. As straight-out male bait, perfume has been enjoying a sensuous success since ancient times, when women of the earliest known civilizations first thought of mixing floral oils, unguents and lotions to wear for the alluring effects such potions had on their prey.

Your perfume wardrobe should include a basic "signature." This would be your favorite perfume, but definitely one that tones in with your personality as a woman. A dark, vivacious, arresting woman, for example, has what it takes to give life to a heady Oriental blend. A fair, shy, gentle person would not— she should use a light floral blend, or perhaps a fresh citrus variation.

234

At the same time, remember that a sexy woman is a woman who understands the element of surprise—so you should have a perfume wardrobe, and change your scent from time to time with the mood, the occasion. A light eau de toilette is just right for a day in the sun; a mysterious, heavier fragrance, for a candlelit dinner party.

Where you use perfume is as important as the using of it. A dab below the ear is not really using perfume. Put perfume on your wrists, in your hair, behind your knees and inside your thighs: all the places that get warm and activate the scent. You can even put a few drops on cotton and tuck the cotton inside your bra.

I have found that putting a lot of perfume on flannel cloth and using it to accent lingerie drawers carries through the same fragrance theme as a part of you. Placing a few drops of perfume on the light bulbs releases the scent throughout the house and sets a mood.

Just never wear perfume itself in the sun, as the oils it contains can cause brown spots on the skin.

Perfume will complete the picture of this glorious you. It's the final touch; don't forget it.

End of Third Week

. . . You did it!

WEIGHT	BUST	WAIST	HIPS	THIGHS

Day XXI

Menu

Breakfast

    1,000 units Vitamin C and 1 therapeutic multiple-
    vitamin capsule with minerals
    1 or 2 slices whitefish

Lunch

    Scallops in red wine

Dinner

    Smoked salmon with caviar
    Stuffed filet of sole
    1 glass of white wine, if desired

* Do not forget eight glasses of liquids!

Scallops in Red Wine

½ lb. bay scallops
1 cup red wine
2 chopped shallots
2 tbs. chopped parsley
¼ tsp. thyme
½ tsp. salt
2 cloves of garlic, chopped
2 tbs. creamed margarine, to which you must add half
   of the chopped garlic

Put the red wine with the shallots, parsley, thyme, salt and half of the chopped garlic in a heavy skillet. Simmer them together for 20 minutes. Add the scallops and cook for 3 minutes, being careful not to allow them to become tough. Remove the scallops from the pan into a baking shell and spread the garlic margarine over them. Brown the scallops quickly under the broiler and eat at once.

Smoked Salmon with Caviar

Cut two thin slices of salmon into 1-inch strips. Spread the strips with black caviar or red Great Lakes salmon eggs and roll them into a cornucopia. Fasten with a toothpick.

Stuffed Filet of Sole

1 filet of sole—washed and dried with paper towels
4 tbs. salad oil
¼ cup canned lobster
⅛ tsp. salt
4 mushrooms, finely chopped
4 tbs. finely chopped parsley
½ tbs. minced onion
⅛ tsp. oregano
1 minced scallion
½ clove garlic, minced
½ tomato, seeded, peeled and chopped
1 tbs. vermouth

Preheat oven to 350°. Mix together lobster, 2 tbs. oil, salt, mushrooms, parsley, onion and oregano. Spread the mixture on the sole and roll the sole. Fasten the fish with a toothpick and place it on a piece of foil. Combine the remaining ingredients, add a pinch of salt and spoon the sauce over the sole. Now fold the foil together and bake for 30 minutes.

Exercise One / To Limber Up

Lie on stomach, forehead touching the floor. Inhale deeply as you reach back and grasp ankles. Extend legs, thus raising the chest and as much of the legs as possible from the floor. Hold for the count of 3 and exhale as you slowly return to starting position. This is a powerful exercise and should be done very carefully to avoid muscle strain. Repeat 3 times and work up to 10.

Exercise Two / For Waist

Sit up straight, hands placed flat on floor just behind hips. Draw knees up to chest, inhaling. Rotate hips to left side, touching knees to floor. Exhale sharply. Pull knees back up to chest and inhale. Repeat exercise to the right. Do it 10 times, each right-and-left movement counting as 1, and work up to 20.

Exercise Three / For Abdomen

Lie on your back on floor, hands clasped behind your head. Inhale. Swing up quickly and pull up your knees at the same time. Exhaling as you do, try to touch both your elbows to the right of your bent knees; then inhale as you return to floor, and exhale as you swing forward and try to touch your elbows to the left of your knees. Repeat 3 times and work up gradually to 20.

Exercise Four / For Calves and Back of Thighs

Stand straight with your feet about twenty-four inches apart, your right foot slightly behind your left. Sink down as slowly as is comfortable on left knee, in a slow lunging fencing movement. Keep your right leg straight. (You may raise your arms if it helps your balance.) Exhale as you lunge forward and inhale as you return to starting position. Repeat 10 times, alternating right and left legs.

Exercise Five / For Waist, Abdomen and Legs

Lie on back on floor, legs together, arms at sides. Inhale as you lift your legs slowly in air. When your legs are raised, start trying to make the capital letters of the alphabet with your feet. Go as far as you can. Breathe in and out as you make the letters. I cannot say how many letters you should make. Make as many as are comfortable. The next time you do this exercise, continue with the alphabet where you left off.

Exercise Six | For Circulation

Stand straight and jog in place. Lift knees as high as you can. Eventually you should be able to raise your knees as high as your chest. Start with 10 times and work up to 20 with each leg, breathing in and out as quickly as you can.

When All Else Fails

Today is the last day, and I've given you lots of beauty tips, all of them adaptable to your own way of life. But let's suppose that you picked up this book at a time when you needed more help to rejuvenate you than I can give. What then? Then you've got to think about another way to beauty. You should start to consider cosmetic surgery if you can possibly afford it.

To this day women recoil in horror at the thought of going to a doctor for cosmetic surgery. A nose or a scar is permissible, but the idea of a breast-lift or a few tricks here and there to remove a chin or two isn't really permissible or discussable.

For the life of me, I can't understand why. If and when I look in a mirror to see that the years have taken their toll to the point at which cosmetics and all the sorcery I can conjure up won't do the job, then I'm going to a plastic surgeon and ask for help. What's the matter with becoming youthful again?

There are many avenues open to the woman who is seeking a more youthful face, and I'm not going into them in great detail. I'll tell you about some of the things that can be done and you'll have to decide whether or not you want or are ready for them.

    1. Silicone can be injected into frown lines or smile

lines. The lines are fairly well filled out and thus eliminated. This process is not without its hazards. I had it done and some of the silicone dripped down to either side of my mouth, leaving little puffs that I just hate. I could have them removed by an operation, but I'd certainly never do that. Silicone can be implanted (not injected) into too-small breasts and for reconstructive surgery after breast removal. This costs about $1,000.

2. Breasts can be lifted if they droop. The cost is again about $1,000.

3. Sagging chins and crepey necks can be pulled back very, very successfully at a cost of about $1,000 each, with maybe a discount for the two at once.

4. Thighs can be trimmed to look firm for about $1,500. But exercise is a lot cheaper.

5. A face-lift that is the ultimate in rejuvenating really furrowed skin costs up to $5,000.

6. A sagging stomach can be lifted for about $2,000. This leaves a thin scar around the waist and I'm told is very painful.

7. Buttocks that droop can be lifted back to youth for about $2,000. This sounds okay to me, for a sagging bottom is a real age giveaway. At the moment I'm operating on the theory that if I keep the back of my thighs very firm I won't face this problem. Only time will tell.

8. There is dermabrasion, a process of planing down the skin so that new skin grows. The cost varies, depending on the number of planings, from $500 to $1,500. I'd be afraid to have this done, because if the planing is too deep the skin looks shiny and very taut. It just isn't worth the risk to me.

9. Eyelids can be unwrinkled for a cost of up to $5,000.

These are but a few of the things that can be done, if and when you need it. The choosing of a plastic surgeon is very important. They're not all good. The top plastic surgeons won't try to sell you anything; they'll tell what they can do and no more. You've got to find your plastic surgeon at one of the top medical centers in your region. For instance, in my humble opinion (and this is only my opinion), New York City has only five centers that I would consider. If I didn't know to whom I wanted to go for plastic surgery I would call each hospital and ask for the names of all the plastic surgeons on its staff. Then I would visit several of these doctors and consult with them. This is, to me, the only way one can decide on a doctor whom one doesn't know.

These few words tell you very little about plastic surgery. It's just a thought I've presented to those who are honestly in need of it. Plastic surgery will not replace the other twenty tips, or diet, or exercise. These are essential components of a more feminine you. Don't ever make the mistake of thinking that plastic surgery will eliminate the need for them. It doesn't pretend to. But it can work miracles for many when all else has failed.

Conclusion

Now that you've finished three weeks of intensive concentration on you and your world of beauty—what now? I'll tell you what now, because I did it and you've got to profit by my experience.

If, indeed, you followed my advice, you've got to be pleased with the results. No matter what shape you were in, you have got to look better now. Are you going to throw it all away? How do you maintain what you've got? How did I maintain what I've got? I'll tell you how.

First of all, I have never given up on my diet. I developed a liking for seafood, and it dominates my diet. However, I now allow myself to eat meat and some vegetables (although I have completely eliminated the most fattening, such as peas, lima beans and potatoes). What I do every day of my life is weigh myself. If I've gained two pounds, I'm really carefully careful. Out goes the meat; away go the vegetables. In other words, I'm forever on guard. I allow myself lapses, but never to the point of undoing my work.

I exercise daily. I try to perfect the exercises that I started. I pick one or two exercises from each group and do them every

251

day. In particular, each Exercise Six is essential every day. The increased circulation will help maintain the youthfulness of your skin and prolong the life of your heart and your other vital organs.

You may not yet have achieved your goal, or you may have the figure you desired. In either case, exercise is here to stay in your life. You'll find that your body will become stiffer and your muscles more slack every day you don't exercise. It's easy not to do it. But you'll lose your feeling of well-being, the extra energy and zip that are a part of you now. You'll start feeling tired—and worst of all, you will have wasted three weeks of your life! I am so worked up and enthusiastic about what I'm doing that I find myself making an extra five or ten minutes a day for more exercises. I'm determined not only to maintain what I've got—I'm going to get better! A better shape means better health, as well as a vastly improved ego.

As for the beauty tricks I learned, I use them. I wear eyelashes and hairpieces. If I come home from work looking as if I'd been in a hurricane, I pull myself back together! My husband, family and friends no longer have to look at a woman who looks beat. I try to look serene and well groomed no matter what happened during the day. Again, it's a great ego stimulator.

You'll notice that I use the word "ego" frequently. Too many people misunderstand the word and construe it to mean vanity. Wrong! Webster says that ego is "self-awareness, the self on which experience is imposed." Why shouldn't your ego have the experience of being admired imposed upon it? It should and it will have this beautiful feeling not just once, but often— if you continue on this marvelous path upon which you have already set yourself.

The sum of

      Beauty
    + Good Health
    <u>+ Self-confidence</u>
    = A more wonderful life.

I've given you this life. Now hold on to it!